IMMEASURABLE LIFE

The Essence of Shin Buddhism

IMMEASURABLE LIFE

The Essence of Shin Buddhism

John Paraskevopoulos

SOPHIA PERENNIS

First published in the USA
by Sophia Perennis
an imprint of Angelico Press
© John Paraskevopoulos 2020

Series editor: James R. Wetmore

For information, address:
Angelico Press
169 Monitor St.
Brooklyn, NY 11222
www.angelicopress.com
info@angelicopress.com

ISBN 978-1-62138-542-4 (pbk: alk. paper)
ISBN 978-1-62138-543-1 (hbk: alk. paper)
ISBN 978-1-62138-544-8 ebook

Cover photography by Neven Bijelić
Graphic design by Laura Silvestri
and Michael Schrauzer

CONTENTS

Foreword ix
Acknowledgments x

PREAMBLE
What is Shin Buddhism? 1
How is this teaching relevant to my life? 2

PART ONE: LIFE
Can the world give me the fulfillment I seek? 7
Why is it so difficult to be content? 11
Is happiness possible in this life? 13
I lead a perfectly normal existence so why do I still feel empty? 15
Isn't love something genuinely meaningful? 17
Why do we suffer so much? 21

PART TWO: REALITY
Can we know what is real? 25
What is reality? 29
Who are we? 33
What is the world? 36
Why are we here? 40
What happens when we die? 43

PART THREE: PRACTICE
What is spiritual practice? 49
How are we transformed? 54
What about my imperfections? 58
How do we entrust? 62
Can I ever become a better person? 66
What does it mean to take refuge? 70

CONCLUSION
A Synopsis of Shin Buddhism 77

Foreword

This short work aims to present the principal teachings of Shin Buddhism in clear and direct language while avoiding, as much as possible, technical terms that might obscure the intrinsic meaning of what it seeks to convey to us.

The founder of this Japanese tradition was Shinran (1173-1263) who sought to bring ordinary people to a consoling awareness of a wonderful all-embracing reality that strives to take us back to itself, which is our real essence. While drawing on the primary doctrines of earlier Buddhism, Shinran gained new insights into the compassionate nature of this reality and its desire to free us from the darkness of our unillumined life.

In order to make the teaching more accessible to a contemporary audience, a 'question and answer' format has been adopted. The questions venture to address concerns that most of us have regarding the pressing difficulties in our lives, with the answers aiming to be lucid and to the point.

The responses presented initially avoid many of the traditional terms employed by Shinran and his predecessors. These will be discussed later in the work because, from the beginning, it is important to understand the heart of this teaching in its most essential and universal form. This will then give the reader a more useful framework for exploring Shin Buddhism in light of its unique understanding of reality and our relationship with it.

Brief passages from the writings of Shinran have been added to the end of each chapter so that readers may gain a sense of his style and spirit. Furthermore, an extensive concluding section is provided that attempts to explore his vision in a little more depth.

It is hoped that, in a world afflicted by distress and angry confusion, Shinran's valuable contribution in shedding light on our most vital human concerns can become better known to a wider audience aching for relief in this time of spiritual crisis.

J.P.
Canberra
Nirvana Day 2020

Acknowledgments

The original impetus for this work was a suggestion from Mr Stephen Lane back in 1995, who threw down the challenge of writing an approachable introduction to Shin Buddhism devoted to the urgent spiritual needs of everyday people. While several attempts were made to meet that requirement without sacrificing depth or rigour, the desired objective was not entirely satisfied in the ensuing years and so this initiative remained idle.

The matter was subsequently rekindled by a recent approach from Mr Bede Draper who urged a resumption of this worthwhile endeavour; in particular, by focusing on how this tradition had the great potential to transform the lives of genuine seekers in the modern world.

Initially, this seemed dauntingly ambitious—or at least beyond the capacities of the author—but owing to the enthusiastic encouragement of Mr Draper, a tentative attempt has now been made in that direction. Without his unflagging assistance and beneficial advice, this book would not have seen the light of day.

I am most obliged to Mr Chris Morgan for sharing a number of astute insights that proved especially valuable in my reflections. Much appreciation is extended to Ms Silvia Viaggio, Ms Barb Mac-Carl and Mr Steve Bastasch for their very helpful suggestions in improving the text. Thanks are also due to my Australian colleagues, Reverend George Gatenby and Reverend Dr Mark Healsmith for their thoughtful advice on this work and for their ongoing support over the years.

Preamble

What is Shin Buddhism?

This is a school of the Buddhist tradition whose teaching is focused on an ever-present reality that pervades our lives with an invigorating wisdom and a lively compassion. It is warm, benevolent and continually working to return us to our timeless home.

Far from being something impersonal or distant, it dynamically reaches out to lift the burden of suffering associated with the often brutal and terrifying conditions of our existence. In doing so, it does not change the way things are but profoundly alters our experience of them so that we're no longer overwhelmed by the severe trials of life.

This can only happen when we become firmly entrenched in its abiding presence rather than in the perishable conditions of this world and the unstable flux that is our broken ego-driven personality. Therefore, our paramount purpose is to become awakened to this boundless reality as a compelling fact in our daily lives.

While we cannot apprehend it through our senses or by thinking alone, a living encounter with this phenomenon leads to a subtle but far-reaching shift in our hearts and minds that impels us to take wholehearted refuge in its truth. It then becomes something that is always available to us as we undergo a powerful transformation that forever changes our outlook on life and death. This is not a question of mere religious belief but, rather, a settled conviction that can be confirmed here and now, even in the midst of great adversity.

When we come under the sway of this loving force, an attitude of deep entrusting spontaneously arises within us. This imparts a spiritual joy to our lives that remains unaffected by the mixed fortunes of worldly happiness. And when the time comes for us to depart, we shall be led to a realm of endless light in which permanent freedom from all suffering is assured.

"My eyes being hindered by blind passions,
I cannot perceive the light that grasps me;
Yet great compassion, without tiring,
Illumines me always."

1

How is this teaching relevant to my life?

If we're being completely honest, we must admit that our lives are not a bed of roses, to say the least. We are repeatedly racked by dissatisfaction yet appear to be, at the same time, totally captivated by life. While harbouring an unfathomable longing for happiness, we quickly find—from a very young age—that it is elusive. Why is such a powerful yearning so difficult to fulfill and why does the way of the world run counter to this fundamental desire we have for a peaceful heart?

Life is a constant struggle with anger, love, fear, desire and hatred not to mention the ceaseless threats posed by our fragile bodies and unpredictable environment. It seems that pain and suffering await us at every turn and never let up. No wonder we come across so much despondency among people for there appears to be a huge chasm between where we find ourselves in life and where we would rather be.

So many of our efforts to rectify these problems strike us as futile because, even if we do succeed for a while in extracting some meagre fulfillment from our daily existence, it is often quickly snatched away from us and we become dismayed again. And so we ask ourselves: What am I doing wrong? Is it just a matter of finding a better life plan? How can I know what will really make me happy?

The reason why this teaching is crucially important is that it points to a durable solution for our predicament. It shows us that what we mistakenly believe is necessary to 'fix' ourselves can never really work and it does this by indicating the true cause of our suffering.

Ultimately, nothing that we generate from our mere thoughts, feelings or actions as limited beings can save us from despair and a sense of meaninglessness. This is because we are much more than just the restricted functions of our mind and body. If we limit the understanding of who we are to this aspect alone then, as the Buddha clearly taught, the only certainties we have left are sickness, old age and death.

These are harsh insights that many of us try to avoid but, unless we face this challenge without evasion, we'll continue to wander aimlessly in a fog of bitterness and perplexity. Our disenchantment in the face of such unpleasant facts may very well be the key to us finally awakening from our spiritual slumber.

Before long, the world will run out of things to give us. We spend our entire lives enclosed within little personalities which will also end up having nothing left to offer. Indeed, we are beset with countless needs that are hard-wired to fail.

If we come to see this flimsy self as all there is, we will frantically aim to preserve it at all costs. Our obsession with propping up our unique identities is therefore a defence against the fear of nothingness that we believe awaits us at death; and, while continuing to live, we seek to artificially strengthen our personalities by projecting onto the world as positive an image of ourselves as possible, even if it is false. This, too, is a protective strategy adopted to deal with the anxiety, hurt and unrest we feel when plunged into the tempestuous ocean of our transient lives.

Self-preservation, then, appears the only way we can resist the looming but dreadful expectation of our non-existence. The fact that we do not have anything on which to rely, in the face of this dire situation, can manifest as a devastating feeling of emptiness.

Satisfaction is commonly thought to come from our loves, sensations, possessions and our general enjoyment of the material world. But we can all agree that our pleasure from these is not lasting. Unfading joy must lie in something that does not depend on any experience generated by the body or mind, both of which will eventually let us down.

Rather than battling with ourselves, resisting the world or reacting against others, we need to fill our being with a reality that is enduring. This will help us to remain firm in the face of constantly changing circumstances. We can only successfully do so when there is diminished reliance on our repetitive psycho-physical existence to give us happiness, for there is no real life in this whatsoever.

To live as a human being is to be hemmed in by innumerable obstacles that frustrate and impede our attempts to flourish in life. The solution, then, is to seek refuge in that which is unconditioned because only this can end our toil in the quest for authentic meaning.

Shin Buddhism proposes a way of life that puts us in touch with what Shinran called the 'true and real'. It urges us to give up trying to improve our personality and to simply rest in the welcoming lap of this reality, just as we are. When enfolded by the source of all being, we experience respite from the tumult of our chaotic minds which flounder in a world without solidity.

Given the many vain attempts to remedy our sorrowful situation, we need to carefully consider what the only resolution to it may be. If what this tradition has to say about it is correct, then the impact on us could be life-changing in that we would, at long last, be given a firm foundation in true well-being.

"The light of compassion illumines us always and the darkness of our ignorance is already broken through. Yet the clouds and mists of greed, desire, anger and hatred always obscure the sky of true faith. But though the light of the sun is veiled by clouds and mists, below them there is still brightness."

Part One: Life

Can the world give me the fulfillment I seek?

There is, of course, nothing wrong with trying to make our lives happier and more fulfilling. It is natural to seek harmless enjoyment wherever we can. So it's not this desire that's the problem.

The difficulty arises when we either cannot get what we want or lose those things we chased after in the belief they would give us happiness, such as a devoted life partner, a rewarding career, good health or enriching friendships. Some even hunger for control and dominance over others despite the adverse consequences this can lead to.

But we can also experience boredom with the goods of life we previously thought essential to our welfare. This can bring about an unsettling anguish—what the Buddha referred to as *dukkha*—as we begin to lose confidence in our judgement regarding what we really need in order to feel complete. We lurch from one unsatisfying experience to another as we desperately try to recapture some thrill that got us excited in the past.

Some desires are perfectly natural while others can be less than wholesome. In either case, we're still trying to do the same thing—filling a void in our lives caused by dissatisfaction or a general world-weariness. The thing to remember, though, is regardless of where we choose to find fulfillment, all of us will inevitably come up against a wall of resistance.

This is because the world, being a coming together of frequently changing conditions, is unable to grant us anything that's everlasting—it simply cannot give what it doesn't have. To the extent we invest all our hopes and energies in that which will eventually pass, we're setting ourselves up for sharp disappointment.

To be sure, we can experience a range of lovely things in life but they are either short-lived or the intensity of their hold on us fades with time. As a result, we then rush off to find something new which we hope will be a little more trustworthy than what has previously let us down.

Alternatively, we may throw our efforts at any number of pressing social or political causes with a view to making the world a better place. This, of course, is perfectly commendable (as long as we're actually improving things and not making them worse) but even then, the results often either fall short of expectations, have unintended consequences that are unwelcome or fail to meet the aspirations of those we were aiming to help. Sometimes, we don't even know what's good for ourselves let alone others.

In the end, though, we simply need to recognise that there are no worldly solutions to spiritual problems and that even the most well-intentioned social initiatives can never bring about heaven on earth. Once we believe that everything of value can be reduced to ideological slogans, all that remains is the joyless pursuit of power and the relentless battle to maintain it—this can only leave us morally impoverished.

Neither the right nor the left side of the political spectrum has a monopoly on the truth. While both believe they are serving the best interests of humanity, the real basis for our spiritual well-being cannot be found in their respective agendas. Such convictions are unable to cure the fierce tenacity that grips a heart consumed by desire and delusion; nor can they help us overcome the worst excesses of our muddled thinking, which fancies that this world of death and uncertainty can afford us any kind of authentic refuge.

This truth also applies to other aspects of our lives. The Buddha would have readily acknowledged that we all need a fundamental level of financial security—much less perhaps than what is often considered acceptable today—in order for our spiritual development to thrive. However, this does not give us licence to lose ourselves in meaningless consumption or striving for more affluence than is necessary to be just comfortable or pain-free.

Surely the purpose of ensuring an adequate level of material stability—or at least as stable as a world such as this can provide—is to allow us the opportunity to pursue higher goals, ideally ones that conform to our true ends as spiritual beings.

While there is much value in the creation of wealth when it serves a noble purpose, we should not consider it an end in itself. Naturally, it is difficult for people to focus on spiritual matters if they are hungry or suffering acutely in other ways. In this respect, sound economic practices can certainly be helpful in meeting our basic wants but, in themselves, possess no intrinsic values that contribute to more enduring forms of prosperity.

Furthermore, many social failings are the result of our own folly which, if not addressed, can often lead to untold cravings being unleashed that then require a vast economic apparatus to assuage them; such as we find in today's world thanks to all-pervasive modern advertising and its peddling of so many unnecessary consumer products.

It is not enough to merely obtain gratification from the various distractions the world can offer, superficially consoling as they may be. In fact, the Buddha pointed out that we would be better off in reducing our desires, the plethora of which lies behind the modern craze for insatiable consumption and the increasing emptiness it creates within us; not to mention the crippling effect of countless addictions to which this gives rise, along with the highly detrimental effects on our physical and mental health.

We are also told that our quality of life can be enhanced by giving greater attention to meditation and ethical exertion, and that this is the contribution that Buddhism can make towards a healthier society. But the Buddha's teaching should not be reduced to just an elevated moral outlook or to heightened powers of mental concentration.

There is not much evidence to suggest, sad to say, that these have helped to change the world for the better. Things are just as lamentable, spiritually speaking, as they have ever been—if not worse in some respects—notwithstanding the countless efforts by so many to perfect such practices. At the end of the day, we may feel greater self-satisfaction in our perceived virtue but are we really wiser or more fulfilled?

We must first engage with our own existential situation before giving any thought to successfully improving things through limited moral, political or economic initiatives. The nature of the world will always reflect the quality of our inner lives so, if this is damaged, we cannot expect to rectify the ills of society by ignoring the root causes.

This will only add more fuel—comprising our unbridled desires and blind attachments—to a world that is already on fire. These flames can be doused only by the soothing waters of enlightened reality, for the proper response to a world of fading pleasures is to submerge oneself in an abiding realm of wisdom and compassion, wherein lies true freedom from all sorrow.

When we seriously consider the matter, we ought to see that it's not the world itself that is blameworthy here but rather our response to it as hurting and confused beings. It's not as though life somehow promised us countless delights for our good pleasure on which it then cruelly failed to deliver. It is we who tenaciously hang on to a false expectation of what our real needs are and how they can be met or, indeed, of how the world is meant to be. This suggests that the problem actually lies at the core of our everyday self.

"The Unhindered Light harbours . . . purity, joy and wisdom;
Its virtuous working surpasses conceptual understanding,
As it benefits beings throughout the ten quarters."

Why is it so difficult to be content?

All that we wish for appears to be without end. We often hear, "If only I had this thing or that person in my life, then everything would be fine. If only I could get over this difficulty or problem, then things would go smoothly again". The reality is that satisfying a desire or avoiding a crisis is only temporary because, before too long, new desires will emerge and other crises will challenge us—it never really ends. We find ourselves constantly grasping for that which will make our suffering go away. And yet it doesn't. Why is this so?

Perhaps it has something to do with the kind of creatures we are and the nature of the world in which we live. The Buddha observed that what makes us up as human beings is inherently unstable. The corporeal matter comprising our bodies is subject to change and decay. Our thoughts, feelings, sensations and memories can also fail us as a result of old age or illness and so these too are destined to pass away.

As if this wasn't enough, we find that the things of this world do not persist either, always arising in a great surge of life only to be blown away by the restless winds of impermanence. So, given this undisputed fact of our existence, why are we so troubled by it?

The answer is that, from the inmost core of our being, we are consumed by a powerful longing for a happiness that can never fade. This remarkable fact about us has no natural or evolutionary explanation.

Given, therefore, that we have this inscrutable yearning in our hearts—while having to endure a world resembling an evanescent mirage and a body that's incessantly breaking down—it should not surprise us that these two components of our experienced life can never measure up to what our deepest need is crying out for.

This is something unique to us seeing as animals are not bothered by such concerns being, as they are, quite content with food, sleep and procreation. What makes us different will become more evident later.

When considered in that light, we quickly come to see that nothing in our world of continual change and loss can address this seemingly inexplicable need. Attempts to extract from the world what we believe will make this longing go away cannot succeed.

Accordingly, one may safely say that living a merely human existence is, literally, hopeless in that we cannot depend on it for our ultimate peace of mind. So, what sense can we make of all this? If we're unable to rely on ourselves or the world for genuine happiness, on what can we really depend? What else is there?

To do justice to this baffling state of affairs, we need to look higher and come to know that there is a true refuge available to us in which we can finally rest—an impregnable sanctuary that we're unable to create for ourselves and which the world is incapable of ever giving us. It is not anything physical, emotional or intellectual and it has nothing to do with either effort or ability.

———————————

"The mind is like a venomous snake or scorpion…
And each of us, in outward bearing,
Makes a show of being wise, good and dedicated;
But so great are our greed, anger, perversity and deceit,
That we are filled with all forms of malice and cunning."

Is happiness possible in this life?

From what we have seen so far, indelible happiness appears to be ungraspable because we are seeking to get it from volatile circumstances or inconstant people. If we believe that the world and its experiences are the key to being fulfilled in life, doesn't it stand to reason that when any of those things change then so will our happiness? And even if they do not change immediately, we have already observed that our own thoughts, preferences and feelings are always shifting and never firm.

So either what we're running after never stays the same (which is what we want it to do) or our own attitude undergoes a reversal such that what previously was desirable no longer is so—either through boredom or just becoming jaded—and thus ceases to give the enjoyment it once did. The lesson here is that both ever-changing objects and fickle subjects can never guarantee a happiness that does not wither.

As much as we may want to resist it, the conclusion is slowly emerging that real happiness must be grounded in something other than our self and its external interests. Of course, this sounds very strange—possibly even shocking—given that we spend our entire lives trying very hard to meet these personal needs in the hope of securing a contented existence. To question this goes against the grain of what many in the world believe makes for a happy life.

One often hears the objection: "How can you say such a thing? My life is deeply enriched by my precious children, my devotion to the arts, helping others, spending time in nature" and so forth. No one doubts that these are wonderful blessings, but we might benefit from the Buddha's reminder that even these can be taken away from us or that our pleasure in them might end suddenly through accident, illness or death.

This is but an honest and clear-eyed view of things as they are, without the sugar-coating that we tend to put on life to make certain uncomfortable truths more palatable.

So where do we go from here? Our choices are either to give up on any kind of secure happiness and learn to live with scraps of momentary satisfaction here and there or to begin looking elsewhere. If we're not prepared to settle for the compromise option, we need to seriously consider that our true thriving may only be found in awakening to that which is not subject to decay and disappointment. In other words, in a reality that is unchanging.

"Ignorance and blind passions abound,
Pervading everywhere like innumerable particles of dust.
Desire and hatred arising out of conflict and accord
Are like high peaks and mountain ridges."

I lead a perfectly normal existence so why do I still feel empty?

The reason for this is that we often confuse functional living (i.e. success in acquiring what's needed to get by in life) with meaningful living. By this, we are alluding to a way of being that is informed by a purpose higher than the demands of our mundane existence.

This explains why even highly-accomplished individuals, who are widely admired or envied for their wealth or fame, can often be plagued by a gnawing sense of sadness which they cannot explain. That's because the emptiness they feel points to an unmet need that exists at a deeper level than their functional life and which is often disguised by an obsessive drive to succeed at all costs.

This is not always apparent to us so we desperately seek increasingly more intense (and often harmful) carnal and emotional encounters, as if to banish the vague but unsettling apprehension that makes us feel so vulnerable. These are poor surrogates for the true fulfillment that is deeply yearned for but which ever remains out of reach.

It appears as though our everyday experience, in chasing after what we think of as 'happiness', only serves to confirm where it's certainly *not* to be found. Given that we tend to suppress this deep longing we feel for something more enduring (because we're often told that it's all just a trick of the mind corresponding to nothing real), we end up acquiescing to false substitutes in all the wrong places.

Our failure in this regard inevitably leads to a painful state of disillusion. However, *dis-illusion* can be a very important teacher in that it dispels many errors and misconceptions regarding how things really are. It helps us to see that what we previously thought reliable in life will eventually start to unravel and show its true colours as something frail and insecure.

Our real dilemma is that our very nature clamours for a lasting fullness. We want, more than anything, to feel complete yet everything we frantically grasp at falls short of what we pine for. And yet, our failure to attain this abundant wholeness does not make our obscure longing go away. Thus we continue to be dissatisfied with life without knowing what to do about it.

Discovering this fact is a critical moment in our lives because it opens a door to the answer for what torments our restless and uneasy hearts. Denial is not a real choice here unless we want to continue living in emotional turmoil as a divided self.

We all seek to sweep this realisation under the carpet—usually by keeping ourselves endlessly 'busy'—so as to avoid its intensely confronting implications but it repeatedly comes back to bite us. It's as though the shallow confidence in our fumbling efforts at happiness is being shaken to its roots so that we may clearly be shown how we've gone off the rails.

When we come to appreciate this truth, it begins to dawn on us that the compelling nature of this powerful yearning—that never leaves us alone—must correspond to a reality that is *spiritual*. In other words, only that which is not subject to our own fragility, or the imperfection of the world, can fully quench this thirst. Why is that? Because there is something of this reality dwelling in our hearts *that is constantly calling us home.*

"Faith is the heart and mind without doubt . . .
free of that which is empty and transitory."

Isn't love something genuinely meaningful?

For very many in this world, love is the most sought-after experience in life. There is no sacrifice too great in the quest to attain it. It is widely seen as the key to happiness to such an extent, that we all must come to terms with it and understand its real nature.

Love ranks as among the most intense and uplifting emotions we can undergo and, yet, it has also caused the most poignant heartache imaginable, leading to hatred, suicide and even murder when it goes wrong. This merely confirms how central it is to most people's understanding of happiness.

So we can agree that this irresistible search for self-completion through loving unions is an extremely powerful force that is difficult to manage; one that can take us to the very summit of exhilaration or bring us down into an abyss of inconsolable despair. Therefore, we ignore it at our peril.

Not all love is the same of course—some is driven by passion (as we find in romantic affairs) while other varieties are based more on affection (the love of parents for their children for example). We also adore nature, works of art and even our pets but there is something particularly fervent in what we observe among people who seek love. So, what do all these instances have in common?

What we find is a desire not to be separated from the person we love. This is because we receive a certain joy from our communion with them that is central to making life worthwhile. For many, it is the only thing that renders our otherwise heart-rending existence bearable. Why does it have this effect?

In some cases, it's because the object of love gives us pleasure, delight or makes us feel good about ourselves. In others, it creates a resilient connection based on an experience of empathy, kindness, strong genetic bonds or deeply-shared values. In any case, what we also find is a most extraordinary willingness to renounce one's own interests—even happiness when necessary—for the object of one's love.

So why does love often turn very badly, usually with ruinous results? What has changed when affections turn sour or are spurned? On the other hand, how is it that love can often withstand the most terrible betrayal?

Perhaps our conventional and all-too-human notions regarding the nature of love might be inadequate in explaining something so important to our lives. Our earlier discussion on desire might hold a clue for us here.

It may be helpful to consider love as a particularly vehement form of yearning which, when it goes astray, can degenerate into infatuation, lust, jealousy or obsession (usually with very unhappy outcomes). In light of our experience of this phenomenon, the tremendous euphoria that we frequently associate with love often feels greater than what any limited object of our affections is able to sustain.

It's as though this impassioned rapture that love elicits is merely *bestowed* on the earthly vehicle with which it is associated, whether it be a special individual, a great musical composition or a breathtaking landscape.

In other words, our everyday loves can be seen as having 'borrowed' their glory from a higher source which, like gentle sunlight, shines on them lending grace and exultation to those encounters that seize our hearts with such longing and devotion.

The fact remains, though, that we often love the wrong things or do so in an improper manner. Our loves usually begin in a flurry of inescapable passion which we feel can never possibly end. Yet they very often do and we become devastated.

There is a feeling of bewilderment about what happened seeing as we were so certain that nothing could ever go wrong. All the same, the love felt was perfectly real although directed to an object that is changeable, just as we are, or confused with something more selfish and degraded.

Buddhists talk about "a finger pointing at the moon" to suggest that we ought to look more deeply into the nature of things and not be satisfied with surface impressions. We see a beautiful shimmering light on the surface of a still pond one evening and think to ourselves "How enchanting!" A bystander then directs his finger towards the moon in order to reveal the origin of the illumination we find so alluring.

In other words, we can see that love is a reflection of something greater that suffuses all things. It's as if we clutch a fragment of it that happens to adorn a person to whom we are attracted which leads us to believe that they alone, in fact, are responsible for those qualities that draw us to them.

But the moonlight can become obscured by clouds or our appreciation of the reflected light may wane, so that our love is apt to dwindle because we fail to see where it can truly be found. This may sometimes lead to a strange sense of betrayal given the initial promise held out by all fleeting temporal beauty.

Love is treasured because it points to the greatest of goods but it cannot be fully contained in the transient things of this world. Even the people to whom we are most devoted will eventually die but does that mean our love for them also fades away? Of course not, which suggests that our affections can live on even if the person evoking them is no longer with us. What we loved about them continues (sometimes more vividly) in a manner not confined to ordinary time and space.

Although unaccustomed to this way of thinking, it may be helpful to consider something so mystifying as a higher reality that embodies all that we most genuinely desire, even though only partial or splintered reflections of it can be encountered here in the dimness of our twilight existence.

Buddhists regard this reality as our ultimate and unfailing object of love which they consider to be eternal, pure, joyous and full of wonder.

"The wish to save all beings is the wish to carry them across the great ocean of birth-and-death . . . it is the aspiration to bring all beings to the attainment of supreme Nirvana; it is the heart of great love and great compassion . . . which arises from the wisdom of immeasurable light."

Why do we suffer so much?

Suffering is the fundamental problem of our existence to which every endeavour is devoted to keeping at bay. It is the result of not getting what we want in life but this is inevitable when seeking total satisfaction in a world where nothing lasts forever. It also arises from ignorance of what lies at the core of who we are.

Our lives are a deluge of unrelenting passions that appear invincible. The Buddha also observed that sickness and death strike everyone and many of us will live long enough to face the bitter infirmities of old age. He also taught how unhappiness shadows the loss of loved ones and the separation of friends, not to mention having to endure the presence of things and people we dislike.

It is a sobering fact that the many hopes we place in our worldly desires and ambitions will remain unfulfilled. As an old adage poignantly reminds us: "Most men lead lives of quiet desperation and go to the grave with the song still in them".

Many will object that this is too pessimistic an outlook on human existence that takes no account of the many joys that distinguish our lives and make them rewarding. As noted earlier, the Buddha never denied these and readily admitted that they were enriching and uplifting.

However, he also observed that regardless of how many marvellous experiences we may have, they never stay the same and must all come to an end. In a sense, the more wonderful something is, the greater the suffering when it is lost to us.

The Buddha once declared, "I teach only about sorrow and the ceasing of sorrow". This was the sole concern of his mission on earth. However, the claim that we can be freed from suffering may strike us as completely unrealistic. How can something so prevalent, that affects every person in the world, be finally conquered?

Many of us would, understandably, say that regardless of how wise the Buddha may have been, he appears to be promising more than he can deliver. And yet, this was an utterly serious claim. He undoubtedly believed that we could reach a point in our lives where suffering cannot touch who we really are.

Yes, we may still be subject to disappointments, sadness and, of course, physical pain but the experience of being overwhelmed by suffering—and having it completely determine how we live in the world—can be overcome.

This is quite different from saying we are guaranteed never to experience anything upsetting or disagreeable in our lives again—that would be unreasonable. Rather, we are taught that there is a dimension in all of us which is immune from the noxious onslaught of what Buddhism calls the *three poisons*: delusion or foolishness; anger or hatred; and greed or selfishness.

This can become something tangibly real for us when we undergo a great transformation in our hearts, as refuge is taken in that which leaves all suffering behind.

The notion of refuge in Buddhism is extremely important and goes to the core of the solution we are seeking to the problem of our deeply-troubled human condition. It calls for an earnest reassessment of how we view ourselves and the world. In other words, we are being forced to question the very things that are thought to bring security and happiness to our agitated lives.

The Buddha tells us that these are a false refuge—because they're ultimately unreliable—and that true shelter from our stormy afflictions is to be found elsewhere. What this is will be considered next.

"In the long night of ignorance, it is the torch:
The wisdom-eye is in darkness, yet do not sorrow.
In the vast sea of birth-and-death, it is the raft:
The hindrance of karma weighs heavy, yet do not grieve."

Part Two: Reality

Can we know what is real?

For many of us, reality is simply the world revealed by our five senses and the inner realm of our imagination, thoughts and feelings. It rarely occurs to us that there might be another way of perceiving that doesn't involve our sight, hearing or sense of touch or that is more than just what our emotions suggest to us.

When we consider how often these ways of knowing lead us astray and create confusion, doubts may arise as to how reliable they are. After all, the senses regularly mislead and our thinking often gets us into trouble instead of bringing us closer to the truth.

Of course, science has proven very effective in providing a largely consistent and predictable view of our universe within certain limits as far as the material world is concerned. But scientific theories are ever being scrutinised and revised in light of new information so complete certainty, even in such an exact discipline, is never assured.

Many things in life continue to perplex us despite all the advances in modern science which, seeing as it isn't concerned with values, cannot impart any significance to human existence; the result being that we will continue to ask questions about life and our place in the cosmos.

When considered with openness and sensitivity, the world ought to provoke a sense of astonishment. We intensely desire to understand why that is because, fundamentally, we are beings who are made to *know*.

Such wonder is not a lack of knowledge or ignorance of real causes but an encounter with a mystery that no acquaintance with the material laws of the universe can help resolve. As we are deeply attracted, even astounded, by phenomena such as love, beauty and grace, we begin to ask ourselves whether there may be some kind of object to which this enigma corresponds.

Our awareness of a hidden dimension to reality that cannot properly be explained by physics, chemistry or biology makes us feel that it has some kind of connection to who we really are. To the extent that there is no living bond with it, we feel somehow incomplete even if every scientific question were to be finally settled.

But how can contact be made with something so unclear and elusive? The Buddha's answer was that we need to employ a different faculty of knowing that is immediate, intuitive and independent of our senses (even though it may use them to see *through* things to what lies behind our earthly phenomena).

The Buddhists call this unique mode of knowledge *prajna* which they distinguish from sense perception, conceptual thinking or emotional judgements, and its emergence in us is frequently associated with images of light and illumination. It is an innate way of knowing but its object remains impenetrable, even though it infuses our life with a feeling of exuberant freedom.

The arising of *prajna* is not the outcome of a logical deduction or scientific experiment and has nothing to do with our calculating ego. This organ of spiritual knowledge—our true centre—is symbolised by the 'heart' which recalls the meaning of *shinjin* ('true heart and mind'), the term used in Shin Buddhism for this awakening that takes place within us.

Though rarely used, this way of knowing is available to everyone even though it may seem rather strange and unfamiliar at first. Even so, it is the only way to get in touch with what is truly real; in other words, with what isn't always passing away, for this reality does not change.

To be receptive to what it can disclose to us, we need to get out of our heads and stop pandering to our disorderly feelings. It is true that we can never completely eliminate our distracting thoughts but we are free to look beyond them, especially once we realise there's a richer way of seeing things which is full of clarity and brightness.

It is understandable, of course, to think of reality simply as the world around us because it's the only one we seem to apprehend. And yet we are painfully conscious of how ephemeral everything is as well as how this affects us deeply, like a permanent wound that will not heal.

Many of us wonder whether there is anything more to existence than what merely comes into being only to vanish so soon. Our instincts tell us that there *must* be something more but we struggle to pin down what it is.

The world reveals phenomena that fill us with awe and we come across people in our lives that leave us deeply moved by their goodness and generosity. Do the qualities embodied in these heightened experiences simply ebb away just because the world always changes? Do we really believe that those we love are nothing more than just a complex bag of chemicals destined to rot in the earth? Perhaps what we're talking about here is intimately linked to this riddle that we are exploring.

On hearing such questions, some might accuse us of not being able to cope with the grim truth that this is how things actually are; in other words, that the true, the good and the beautiful are just a subjective fantasy with no basis in anything unchanging. Thinking otherwise, they would say, is to 'flee from reality'. One wonders, though, who is really running from the truth and lacking in imagination.

We live, without doubt, in an age where everything is up for grabs. Little is taken for granted and nothing is spared from the most savage scepticism. This has had a harmful effect on our lives because it shatters the nourishing confidence that many once had in 'something more'.

Yet despite this, the fundamental sense that we have of life's higher purpose has proven difficult to eradicate altogether and will persist as long as we remain true to the human spirit and its quest for unity, wholeness and harmony.

What emerges, when we are open to something greater than ourselves, is a lively awareness of an inspiring strength in our lives that gives us comfort, peace and rest. Not only does it confer *genuine* wisdom (which has no basis in the ego) but we also discover that it is far from uninvolved in our well-being.

This is evident in both the guidance and unconditional compassion shown to us as we awaken to its active working, which seeks to deliver anguished beings from a false life.

One can endlessly argue back and forth as to whether such a belief is rationally justified but, short of a lucid encounter with it, our uncertainty will remain and we'll continue to feel lost. There is, in the end, no substitute for this powerful transformation that mellows our hardened hearts and raises our spirits when we come under the sway of its wondrous presence.

"Nirvana is called extinction of passions, the uncreated,
peaceful happiness, eternal bliss, true reality . . .
it fills the hearts and minds of all beings."

What is reality?

Most of us have heard of *Nirvana*—often associated with the Buddha's experience of enlightenment—but the concept is difficult to fathom and has caused much confusion.

In every school of Buddhism, Nirvana is considered the ultimate good because it is free from all turmoil and unease although it's most assuredly not a negative state of 'nothingness' as is often incorrectly supposed. This is the final goal we ought to pursue because it remains the only thing capable of satisfying our inmost aspiration for complete freedom and the highest happiness.

While we cannot say too much about an experience that is extremely difficult for our minds to conceive, the traditional characteristics of Nirvana are said to be 'eternity, bliss, purity and true self'. Its realisation also spells the end of all the thirsty craving that fuels our voracious desires and attachments which cause us so much grief. In this sense, Nirvana is something we enter into and touch directly—it's not just an idea we can ponder over as it has nothing to do with thinking.

Later in the Buddhist tradition, this non-dimensional reality came to be seen as the ultimate foundation of existence, also known as the *Dharma-Body*. It is the underlying unity behind all things whose living presence within us comprises our real self that endures beyond our short-lived bodies and identities. Shinran insisted that this reality was inconceivable yet it is the light by which all things are seen and illuminated.

The extraordinary richness of terrestrial life with its countless teeming phenomena is a reflection of the abundantly overflowing spiritual energy of the Dharma-Body. As a consequence of its infinite potential, it pours forth as the boundlessly varied appearances that we find in nature and among living beings.

By unfolding itself in this way, the Dharma-Body necessarily assumes forms that are impermanent and fragmentary, this being the price to be paid for the manifestation of finite things which must involve some privation of a higher perfection. The reality of earthly misery is an explicit consequence of living in a broken world, because only that which is eternally uncorrupted can be free from the oppression imposed by the mutable conditions of our existence.

Consider our sun. Heat and light emanate from it naturally without being willed into existence. Living things benefit enormously from its radiance but do we condemn the sun for some of the unwelcome effects of its energy such as fires, blindness and skin cancer? These are unavoidable consequences of its powerful spontaneous outflow without which nothing would exist at all.

The Dharma-Body is *transcendent* in the sense that it cannot be identified with the world of the senses or the intellect; that is, it lies beyond anything we can grasp with either of these faculties. At the same time, it is also *immanent* in that it dwells in all things and so can be experienced by us here and now.

We come to view it as the font of all goodness and beauty in life, of which we see and pursue only the elusive traces in this dream-like existence that can never bestow the full measure of these blessings to us. Indeed, it is as if every conceivable joy that we could possibly experience has been gathered together and densely concentrated into a single essence that never diminishes.

This is what allows us to gain an awareness of its presence (through that part of us which shares in its nature). To put it another way, we gradually come to know this reality as the very act of it revealing itself in us.

Furthermore, because the Dharma-Body is not apart from anything, it is also that which unites us to each other such that to harm one sentient being is to damage one's own self. In this sense, we are creatures of paradox who while living a finite terrestrial life are joined, inexplicably, to a dimension that is unlimited. This, in essence, is the real cause of all human dissatisfaction but also the reason why complete deliverance from our plight is possible.

Though we are heavily stricken by binding desires that continually inflame our hearts, we have available to us—at the same time—the refreshing serenity of a light that permeates our false self and is the very key to the final liberation of all beings.

What is reality?

Another crucial insight that emerged later in Buddhist thought was that this reality is far from indifferent towards us. In other words, it is *not impersonal* but neither is it burdened by the severe constraints that characterise ordinary human personality. This became a potent experience for those who heard the Buddha proclaim that it seeks to actively save all beings, roused by an unyielding desire to bring our suffering to an end.

In the Buddhist scriptures, this compassionate impulse is known as the *Primal Vow* in that it represents its fundamental will to emancipate us from our grievous predicament. 'Primal' (from the Latin *primus*) denotes that which is of first importance and, of course, 'vow' means a solemn promise, pledge or commitment. In the same way that the disposition of fire is to burn, the essence of the Primal Vow is its desire to draw us into itself.

This insight into its nature was no mere speculation but emerged from an immediate experience of this reality disclosing its presence—for those receptive to its call—in a manner that can readily be recognised.

In its dynamic aspect, the reality behind this benevolent will came to be known as *Amida*, the timeless Buddha, whose name is derived from the original Sanskrit term for that which is incalculable and without measure. The presence of Amida is made evident to us as a revealing light that governs and guides our lives by means of a new life that is conferred on us. This awareness cannot be brought about by any self-willed initiative on our part—it can only be *received*.

How is this related to the notion of God? Of course, there will be some similarities. Amida resembles those features of theistic belief that emphasise the merciful nature of the divine which seeks the never-ending happiness of all beings. However, Amida is not wrathful, capricious or vengeful. This reality can only be loving and, as such, should never be approached with fear.

Neither is Amida seen as an all-powerful being that intervenes in the affairs of the world, capable of eliminating things like wars, earthquakes or disease. As mentioned earlier, given that everything in our existence is fleeting, this world can only be host to imperfections and all the ordeals that follow in their wake.

In other words, Amida is not the 'Creator'—it would certainly not want to deliberately bring into being a cosmos as full of calamity as this one; rather, it only seeks to urgently rescue us from it.

And yet this world is contingent on a higher reality from which it has proceeded; this is why goodness, truth and beauty can still shine through to reach us here despite the menacing shadows that frequent our lives.

The main difference is that Buddhism sees this and other particular worlds as coming into being through a series of causes and conditions brought about by *karma*; that is, intentional and (in our case) largely misguided moral actions from previous lives which have led to us being bound to realms of impermanence and tribulation.

And yet, despite our unfortunate situation, we have enough advantageous karma from the past to make us recognise that help is freely available to enable our return to where we truly belong. We simply cannot reach this destination on our own for the darkness in which we are steeped cannot disperse itself.

"The 'Realm of Bliss' is that Pure Land of happiness where there are always countless joys and never any suffering mingled with them."

Who are we?

The question of what makes us who we are has been the subject of serious reflection and passionate debate since thinking beings walked the earth. Opinions have ranged from us being essentially spiritual beings to nothing more than clumps of dirt with a brain. How should we think of ourselves in a way that does justice to our real complexity?

From what we have seen earlier, it is distressingly apparent that our bodies are destined to break down. Whether we die young or in old age, the destiny of our 'mortal coil' remains the same. In fact, our physical make-up is subject to all manner of deterioration from the very moment of our conception.

Despite the exceptional advances in modern medicine that have improved people's lives enormously, we have yet to find a way to cheat ageing and death.

What about our feelings, memories and emotions, not to mention our intellectual powers? Don't they determine who we are? Yes, they are indeed fundamental to the personality that makes us unique individuals but—just like our bodies—these too change, grow dim and lose their integrity even though we can't apprehend them with our senses.

Buddhism teaches that there are five principal components to who we are comprising our body, sensations, perceptions, mental activity and consciousness, the last being the basis of all our experience. These play a key role in the attachments and appetites that disturb us in life and thus determine our way of being in the world.

To the extent that we completely identify with these unreliable elements of our existence, we are said to be driven by the ego-self for which we pay a heavy price in suffering.

So, despite their marvellously intricate nature, it seems that neither our bodies nor minds are terribly durable. Indeed, they are the cause of much trouble throughout our lives. This has led many to believe that there is nothing more to us than our momentary personalities and that we cannot expect anything to survive death.

Shinran's view was very different. While readily admitting that—as ordinary beings—we are subject to continuous dangers, he did not consider the personality as our true self. Therefore, the destruction of our bodies and the loss of our minds does not spell the end of who we really are.

Our true self, then, must be quite different to that which falls apart. It also has to be of the same nature as that which we considered earlier as the object of our deepest longing. Otherwise, there would be no explanation for why the limitations of our personality and its environment leave us so dissatisfied when we desperately clutch at them in the hope of gaining some stability and freedom from want. In other words, this ultimate reality must also reside at the core of our being.

The tradition calls it *Buddha-nature*, something much deeper than the ego and its changeable components (which are particular and unique to ourselves). We are talking here about a universal presence, the same in all beings, that fortifies us spiritually regardless of what the world may throw at us. As the knowing aspect of Buddha-nature, *prajna* is the faculty by which we are able to see the inner unity of all that exists.

This allows real transformation to take place in that our insecure sense of self—by coming under the irresistible sway of this presence within us—finally attains real independence from the domination of external events.

The Buddha considered most of us gravely ignorant of our true state. This is evident from our rash pursuit of bogus substitutes which fall far short of lasting satisfaction. Indeed, this is a sign of the unfulfilled Buddha-nature in all of us and no amount of denial or frenzied distraction can ever really cover it up.

Having always remained with us as an undying reality, we cannot produce this indwelling nature through any kind of personal achievement. All we can do is remain open to its benign influence as it penetrates the thick husk of our ego and gently softens it.

Who are we?

When we surrender to this quiet grace, we come to discover the essence of spiritual personhood, which is non-individual unlike our fluctuating 'personality' that is fated to pass.

The quest for who we really are lies at the heart of this liberating wisdom. Our love and yearning for it is not merely an intellectual pursuit but a response to the beckoning call of ultimate reality, whose inexpressible yet steadfast compassion makes us come to know it as limitless light and unending life.

"Nirvana is called Buddha-nature.
Beyond our ability to attain it in the state of foolish beings,
We will realise it on reaching the Land of Peace."

What is the world?

Ask almost any person on the street and they'll tell you, understandably, that they consider this world to be 'home'. We are born here on the earth just as we are destined to leave it and, in the meantime, find ourselves entirely absorbed by its vast array of sights, sounds, people, places and ideas in all their bewilderingly rich variety.

Our hunger for love, excitement and adventure steers our gaze outwards while, at the same time, we scramble to gratify our relentless physical needs which are often so burdensome. And yet, for the most part, we give the appearance of feeling quite comfortable in the world. After all, what choice do we have? Do we know of any other place to which we can compare it?

It is obvious that the world is everything to us, not only the good things but the bad. There's a sense in which we've already reached an uneasy accommodation even with its tragedies and traumas. Our identity is so deeply wrapped up in the very fabric of our everyday environment that we feel naturally drawn to make it the best possible world we can—a good, just, fair and beautiful place where everyone can live in harmony with each other.

Efforts to achieve this honourable ambition continue unabated although with mixed results and precarious outcomes. One cannot help but feel that we have an image of perfection in our minds that we seek to impose on a world that appears to resist our best efforts and designs. Where does this notion come from? How is it that we come to aspire for a way of being that is free from suffering?

We have seen that the Buddha saw human life as a realm of alienation and ceaseless wants but also as an arena in which one could discover ultimate truth. Indeed, he thought it was only in a world such as this that genuine awakening was possible—any place too pleasant would lead to spiritual indifference whereas conditions even worse than ours would completely distract us from our quest for this truth.

In other words, our life here seems to have just the right balance between joy and hardship to keep us motivated in seeking transcendence while, at the same time, preventing us from feeling too comfortable in this world.

Shinran's entire spiritual focus was grounded in a reality surpassing our incomplete condition but which is also found in all things. As mentioned earlier, when considered in its personal aspect it is known as *Amida* and, when seen as the perfect blissful realm of eternity, it is called the *Pure Land*—a more positive and tangible way of referring to Nirvana.

Samsara is the name given to the entire cosmic process of 'birth and death', the coming and going of beings in an interminable cycle of transmigration. Not only is our world caught up in this process of perpetual change but so are many other non-human realms with their own beings, ranging from the celestial to the infernal. Yet all these worlds—which are equally impermanent—serve the aim of allowing their inhabitants to eventually fulfill their spiritual destiny in the Pure Land of utmost happiness, to which we ever seek to return.

As this reality dwells deep in our hearts, we hanker for the perfection of which it reminds us even though we are rarely attentive to it in our daily life. In a sense, we unwittingly strive to recreate this Pure Land here on earth as if to reflect its tranquil blessedness in the midst of our turbulent world where happiness is always slipping through our fingers.

So while our concerted attempts to eliminate pain and iniquity are most necessary and laudable, they can never fully succeed because, after all, this is not our true home and can never become so. We see so much energy and emotional investment poured into, for example, 'saving the planet' that one can be forgiven for thinking that the earth itself has become the ultimate reality whose interests we must now pursue as our highest good.

By all means do what you can to cherish and protect the world in which you live but never forget that there are limitations to what can be achieved in what is but a flawed and passing abode. And so, we should avoid taking refuge in the deceptive comfort and security that it affords. This is because, despite its many delicate beauties and fragile joys, it remains a shadowy reflection of something much greater and everlasting.

The only way we can tackle our human response to suffering is through wisdom, not radical social reformation or revolutionary political ideas which can never really transform us. Nonetheless, we should—unquestionably—devote ourselves to achieving greater equity in our relations with others by, at a minimum, reducing some of the more deplorable forms of unfairness that serve to undermine civic trust and good-will.

Yet this is not the same as securing true well-being which is the sole concern of the Buddha's teaching. Even so, relationships with others will naturally flourish if we sincerely seek refuge in Amida whose command over our hearts will surely resonate in our interpersonal affairs.

Buddhism reminds us that all life ends in death. Therefore, chasing after an array of fugitive and unfulfilling pleasures is not to live authentically as it dishonours the sacred purpose of our human state through the pursuit of unworthy ends.

This means, among other things, avoiding the spiritual vanity of uto-pianism and the belief that if we only had, say, the right economic policies in place, we could turn our world into a paradise. The often self-righteous belief in human perfectibility betrayed by such wishful thinking ignores the Buddha's unambiguous teaching regarding the reality of samsara and its inherent defects.

When this teaching is properly understood, we find that the state of the world cannot altogether be improved by merely rectifying life's erratic unpredictability through vulnerable social arrangements that appear to suit whatever our worldly interests happen to be at any one time.

In the rush to make Buddhism relevant in an increasingly secular age, we find that it is often used in the service of profane ideologies which are—in so many ways—the bane of our lives today. These must be made subordinate to the reality of life as observed without rose-coloured glasses.

What is the world?

We need to balance our tendency towards unwarranted idealism with the often harsh observations that arise from a realistic perspective on the human condition. The desire to improve the world, while totally commendable, cannot simply be brought about by ordinary thinking or willing.

It must be based on a spiritual realisation of truth which is possible only on an individual, not a collective, basis. Ideological perspectives do not offer any permanent solutions to the 'three poisons' or the predicament of ageing and death; indeed, they can more often be the problem than the solution to the difficulties we face.

Our true ends must reflect our interior life when we have truly sought asylum in Amida. We hasten to satisfy the unceasing demands of our bodies but, as these are material in nature, the persistent longing we feel still lingers because the limited means we resort to will always fail to address the needs of our true self. These can never be adequate solutions unless we're prepared to think beyond the insatiable claims of our senses and emotions which, of course, have a rightful place in life when viewed in a correct light.

Before we take on the colossal task of improving the ailing condition of society, we must first acknowledge the wreckage of our own human nature. To the extent that we continue to live, unavoidably, as ego-fuelled beings, we all contribute directly to the disorder that surrounds us.

That which is inherently prone to being fractured in the external world cannot forever be restored through the mere efforts of those who are also, incurably, flawed in themselves.

_____

"The light of wisdom exceeds all measure,
And every finite living being
Receives this illumination that is like the dawn,
So take refuge in Amida, the true and real light."

Why are we here?

Any reflective person will, during some point in their life, ask this question. We have no say in entering this world or the conditions in which we find ourselves. The fact that our short lives are bounded, on either side, by an immense expanse of seeming nothingness must give us cause to seriously ponder.

If we can just, but momentarily, break the spell of commonplace life and its whirlwind of unabated distractions, we will come to see how peculiar our existence really is.

Regardless of whether our lives are going well or not, the very fact of our being here remains enigmatic. We could just as easily not have been born; indeed, the *non-existence* of our world would have been much less remarkable, especially if we believe that this is all there is.

Many just accept this life as a brute fact having no significance whatsoever. It is often heard that we emerged from dust only to return to it; we somehow came from nothing and this is all that awaits us in the end. But, surely, the utterly stupendous nature of existence—with all its intriguing marvels—cries out for an explanation.

One can't help but feel that those who play down the astonishing spectacle that is life are burying their heads in the sand or are somewhat insensitive to how confronting this mystery really is. Why is there something rather than nothing and not just any 'something' but a reality that is quite astounding in its complexity? How can one casually accept the notion that the staggering profundity of human consciousness, for example, simply appeared out of a blank void?

Perhaps there is not much more that can be said to those who remain unconvinced of a hidden relevance behind the appearance of our world. Therefore, we will only concern ourselves with those for whom this conundrum is very real and who seek a satisfying response to the riddle of existence.

Relying solely on our unaided reason to find the answer will not suffice. What we require is guidance from an unfailing authority in whom we can place our trust. The Buddha was considered such by millions of his followers and his influence continues to this day.

What made him exceptional was not that he was just another philosopher or wise individual but that, through his extraordinary awakening, he saw into the depths of reality. But how is it that anyone could gain such an insight?

As the Buddhist tradition developed over time, many devotees came to see that the founder was not just a typical person but, rather, someone who had access to a wisdom that far exceeded mere worldly knowledge and opinion. How was this possible?

According to Shin Buddhism, the Buddha became awakened to a reality of which he himself was a direct manifestation. In other words, he was the earthly embodiment of Amida—the measureless Light and Life that pervades the universe—who had to manifest a human form in order for his message to be conveyed to the world.

The powerful impact that this had in transforming so many lives is precisely what led to the complete confidence placed in the Buddha's other insights to which his followers had no immediate access.

While the Buddha taught many different doctrines during his 45-year ministry, he gave particular focus to the type of teaching that was especially suited to ordinary beings who required the most help in order to see the truth. So, according to Shinran, what did the Buddha realise as a result of his great awakening regarding our ultimate purpose? *That we need to encounter what is 'true and real' in this life.*

After an unimaginable period of transmigration throughout realms of birth and death going back many lifetimes, we are now faced with the chance to finally abandon ourselves to this vigorous wisdom and compassion that is active in our lives. When we do so, our shiftless spiritual wandering comes to an end.

Therefore, to be born in this 'world of endurance', as the Buddha called it, is not just a random occurrence without any relevance or consequence—it is no mere cosmic accident.

Our lives do have a compelling meaning which is to seize the opening —presented by our rare human birth—to finally escape our samsaric exile. So, to answer our initial question, we are here to rediscover the path that will take us back to our spiritual origin.

———————————

"The light of purity is without compare.
When a person encounters this light,
All bonds of karma fall away;
So take refuge in Amida, the ultimate shelter."

What happens when we die?

Even those who believe in some kind of afterlife tend to think that the person they are now will simply persist—as an ongoing 'soul'—into a future existence in another realm. Buddhists do not question what we ordinarily think of as a soul but deny that it continues on evermore as essentially the same individual that lived here in this world, albeit in a different guise. This is what is more commonly understood as reincarnation which the Buddha explicitly rejected.

If, as observed earlier, the five constituents of our existence (comprising body and mind) are dissolved at death, isn't that simply the final end of who we are? Well, yes and no. The distinct person you are now will certainly no longer exist in its current form—that includes your physical form, thoughts, feelings and memories—because these are ephemeral.

The Buddha taught that what has been fashioned by transient causes and conditions must perish when the momentum that brought them into being has been exhausted. And yet the karmic stimulus that impelled the appearance of a new person in this world continues beyond the particular form of any one individual once it passes away.

So, while someone's body and mind may disappear at death, the energy that forged them will seek to become embodied in a new life in order that the unfolding of its karmic potential can continue—in the form of new short-lived elements—until it reaches its natural terminus which is the end of transmigration altogether.

So there is clearly some kind of continuity between lives but not complete identity. The passage of beings from one world to another is entirely influenced by the extent of their unresolved karma. At the time of death, one's life force or energy is unleashed once again which brings about the formation of a new individual elsewhere.

Ours is the only realm in the Buddhist cosmos that is human and—given that it is a 'central' state which provides the most favourable occasion for exiting the wearisome round of birth and death—there is no guarantee that we will find ourselves here again anytime soon if this opportunity is dissipated.

The Buddha stressed that attaining human birth is a highly exceptional occurrence and thus a precious chance that ought not to be
thoughtlessly squandered. As all realms are subject to impermanence
(including heavens, hells and other spirit worlds), our aim shouldn't
be to aspire for a more pleasant rebirth or come back as a human
being but to abandon these states altogether and attain Nirvana
which, alone, is without suffering.

If a particular individual does not survive from one life to the next,
why should I care what happens to me when I die? Because, in not
seeking emancipation in this life, you will perpetuate further suffering
by contributing to the formation of another being that will continue
to suffer, in turn, because of negative karma that has yet to be resolved.

So we are, indeed, talking about a new person but one whose existence has been conditioned by choices and actions made by you in
this life. Therefore, the two are inextricably linked, in the same way
that a flame is transferred from one candle to another—a new light is
created in a different form but the essence of the previous light continues as well. If you are motivated by compassion you will want to
end, not only your own suffering, but that of other beings to which
your present karma will give rise in subsequent lives.

So what, then, is karma? The word simply means 'action' or 'deed'
and refers to the impersonal law of cause and effect that governs the
consequences of our moral intentions. It is the principle that influ-
ences the nature of our existence—not only our habits and way of
perceiving things but also aspects of the material world.

However, it does not govern every event in our lives and thus has
nothing to do with fate or destiny. There are other causes in the universe that are unrelated to human karma and so life is not entirely
determined. Given that we always retain our free will, despite the
many constraints under which we labour, it continually remains
open to us to make choices that improve our lives and strengthen our
spiritual orientation.

The importance of the doctrine of karma is that it doesn't restrict our
chances for enlightenment to one lifetime only. Some people's lives
are so marred by abuse, cruelty or neglect that they are barely in a
frame of mind to cultivate any kind of inner life. Others are so caught

up in the daily struggle to survive and feed their families that opportunities to pursue anything beyond making ends meet, and just getting through each day, are a luxury.

This is not to suggest that those towards whom life has been pitiless are incapable of spiritual progress; often, dire situations can provoke a deep awakening that might not have been possible otherwise. Nevertheless, it remains the case that many go to the grave brutalised and shattered, resistant to any higher dimension that life has to offer.

Even if someone does show great spiritual promise, their lives can be suddenly cut short in the bloom of youth without their full potential having been realised. It hardly seems fair, then, that no other possibility can be afforded to such unfortunate individuals to continue their journey under more auspicious circumstances.

A common criticism of karma is that it somehow blames the victim for whatever misfortune has befallen them. This misconception fails to recognise that the being who generated the unfavourable karma in a previous life was a different person with their own free will. So whatever has been inherited, karmically speaking, can be improved by actions taken in this life which are the only ones for which anyone can rightly be held responsible.

Those who adhere, instead, to the doctrine of reincarnation believe that it is the same individual or 'soul' who is responsible and thus their misery in this life is viewed as necessary to expend the bad karma they have created. This understanding can result in a lack of sympathy and compassion for a suffering person because they are seen to have 'deserved' what they're going through now. The Buddhist response does not apportion any kind of blame but seeks only to help us all withstand our obstacles in attaining liberation.

It may seem unjust to have to be lumbered with the repercussions of someone else's misdeeds but because a different being was responsible does not change the fact that we are talking about a *single* stream of consciousness that assumes different forms over many lives and with which we are very much implicated.

In the end, though, our final objective remains the perfect joy that awaits us in Nirvana. This is something that, in our tarnished state, we cannot fully appreciate in this life even though deep stirrings within us afford a glimpse of what it might be like, especially when we encounter Amida's 'true heart and mind' (*shinjin*) as our real self.

What is finally liberated in Nirvana is our very own Buddha-nature which, although now heavily encrusted with so many impurities, still allows Amida's serene light to shine through whenever we give ourselves up to it.

Think of a vast assortment of different bottles in the ocean that are full of water. Some are very thick and sturdy while others are quite fragile. The latter are less impervious to the sun and other elements thus making them more likely to crack. When they do, the glass breaks apart and the water inside the bottles rejoins the ocean.

The ocean represents Nirvana and the water in the bottles—which comprises the same substance—is our Buddha-nature 'trapped', as it were, in a vessel (our mind-body complex) that keeps it from being restored to its unconditioned state. So the more our sense of the ego self is reinforced and hardened (i.e. the thicker the bottle glass), the more difficult it will be for the water within to be released.

That part of us which is entwined with the highest reality is all that can really survive unto eternity because it remains the only dimension of our being that is deathless. This is not heaven as is commonly understood by many. Even this realm and its long-lived beings—who remain individuals—must pass away as they too are sustained only by the conjunction of momentary causes and conditions (despite these being formed by 'good' karma which still remains limited by having its origin in us).

Nirvana is inconceivably blissful and bereft of anything that perishes or brings sorrow. This is our original state to which we can—and eventually will—return by entrusting to Amida, the personal and compassionate aspect of this ineffable reality that actively seeks to bring us back to where we undeniably belong.

"When foolish beings possessed of blind passions attain birth in the Pure Land, they are no longer bound by karmic fetters. . . . That is, without severing blind passions, they realise Nirvana."

Part Three: Practice

What is spiritual practice?

In practically all belief systems, practice is viewed as something we need to do in order to either improve our attitude and conduct or to reach a state of being that is attuned to a higher reality. This has often led to aspirations towards perfection based on a religious idealism that is widely held today.

As a result, there arose the view that we must count on our own strength, wisdom and ability to surmount the hurdles that get in the way of spiritual progress. By correcting our characters and confused thoughts, we are seen to become worthy of our lofty vocation.

A problem often encountered by practitioners who adopt this outlook is that they are never quite certain when enough has been done to guarantee success. How much discipline is sufficient to ensure the levels of purity or awakening required to attain one's goal?

In some traditions, this difficulty is particularly acute given that complete reliance on our own efforts is expected. This is because anyone who genuinely tries this, quickly comes up against their immovable limits as a human being. All manner of distractions, temptations and other disturbances will inevitably assault us causing frustration and misgivings regarding our abilities.

Other traditions attempt a compromise whereby considerable effort is still required but access to assistance from a supernatural source is also available. So, rather than resorting to an exclusive self-power approach, this method envisages a form of co-operation in which a working together of both practiser and divine reality are considered necessary.

Once again, we're confronted by doubts regarding what's expected of us in light of our shortcomings and the extent to which we must lean on external support. There is a confounding ambiguity here in that we are never too sure if and when we're ever able to fulfill our end of the bargain by meeting this help 'half-way', so to speak.

Earlier in his life, Shinran was a monk who subjected himself to very demanding ascetic practices for 20 years. During this time, he came to see the problems (including self-deception and hypocrisy) caused by these kinds of striving endeavour in response to which he eventually left monastic life and developed seminal insights that revolutionised how practice was understood in Buddhism.

He discovered that ordinary beings saddled with an ego fuelled by insatiable addictions are unable to accomplish purifying practice. A finite self weighed down with so many restrictions cannot prevail unless taken in and transformed by a reality that remains unsullied.

A being that is only a composite of feeble flesh and insubstantial thoughts will never generate that which is infinite, for this cannot be produced by anything our bounded self can possibly muster. Neither can we earn sufficient 'merit' to somehow make us worthy of it for these two orders of reality are poles apart.

It is these difficulties that led Shinran to conclude, after many arduous trials, that nothing of which we are capable can lift us out of our defensive enclosure of vanity and self-importance.

Unless, as a result of spiritual maturity, we are open to being approached and prompted by this reality to abandon ourselves to its working, we will remain cut off from its life-enhancing graces. This can only lead to isolation, dismay and insecurity which, in turn, causes us to repress these reactions (because they are too painful to bear) or project them onto others in an act of denial.

The force behind this inviting reality mentioned above is known as *Other-Power*. As mentioned earlier, we are not suggesting that there's no place for our own skill and abilities in negotiating the complexities of the world (i.e. functional living) but this kind of competence cannot produce spiritual realisation. Neither does aptitude in intellectual or artistic pursuits have any bearing on our capacity to generate wisdom and approach the transcendent, for it alone can draw us close to it.

Shin Buddhists often experience Amida as a soft yet liberating light that meets us in whatever condition we happen to find ourselves. The crucial transformative encounter between us—just as we are in all our ruptured humanity—and Amida is known as *nembutsu*.

This is made possible by a process of 'deep hearing' whereby we come to realise that we're objects of a fathomless will that seeks to set us loose from the vice-like grip of samsara.

When this all-embracing spiritual momentum breaks through into our lives, and we respond to its call, we undergo a pronounced change at the core of our being (*shinjin*). This helps to elevate our human condition to something more than just never-ending unhappiness and resentment.

The form that this response takes is our invoking of Amida's name with gratitude and a full appreciation of its significance. This is the embodiment both of our taking refuge and the simultaneous expression of the active presence of this immeasurable life working within us.

Vestiges of Buddha-nature can be found even within the darkest of hearts. Contemplating the teaching with reverence will slowly gather together these traces of light to form enough of an opening for this name to be heard as Amida's merciful command to have us entrust ourselves.

This brings us to some reflections on the unconventional nature of Shinran's view on practice mentioned earlier. Following many years of honest and ruthless introspection, he came to see that any practice that leads us to the 'true and real' has to be undertaken by that reality itself.

In other words, *we* do not truly practice but, rather, *are practised* by Other-Power.

What this means is that Amida vowed to take on the work required to transform us spiritually in this life and to bring about our attainment of Nirvana in the next. There is nothing we can add to this process other than a willingness to remain open to the compassionate intrusion of this luminous awareness.

Creatures racked by the three poisons of greed, hatred and foolishness cannot lift themselves out of the mire. We are so shackled by heavy chains of delusion that we have no clue as to how to relieve our lamentable situation.

Unless Amida's light breaks through and penetrates our hearts, we will continue to be clogged up with doubt and perplexity. It may not seem that we are in such a bad way when we reflect on our everyday blessings along with the loving people we have in our lives. And yet, our minds are still seething with concealed 'snakes and scorpions' as Shinran reminds us.

This becomes apparent when we candidly reflect on our selfish desires, vanity, foolishness and the untold ways in which we seem to hurt others and ourselves. These are the inevitable actions of a clouded mind when severed from this light that unveils our true nature.

As we become illuminated by Amida's working, it is as though a spotless mirror is presented before us so that we may see who we are—without distortion—for the first time and to realise the dispassionate nature of that which allows us to have this insight.

Initially, this is very confronting because it forces us to face up to our ugly side, but we cannot properly come to terms with it in any other way; that is, we need to be *shown* what we are because it is impossible for darkness to shed light on itself. According to an old Chinese Buddhist proverb, "We cannot see the dust all around us until the sun is shining".

However, Shinran observed that, while initially disturbing, this revelation of our true nature as unenlightened beings actually gives us a joyous release from our spiritual alienation, which markedly raises the tone of our lives. Once we're made aware of this, we are no longer determined or absorbed by our anxieties and discontent.

We experience perfect freedom in that which surpasses our ego, which then seems very small to us. It continues to be troublesome, of course, but it can no longer harm us for it changes into a snake without fangs rather than remaining the poisonous serpent it once was.

This is what true practice leads to—nothing less than a complete revolution in our hearts and minds—but it cannot be accomplished by us alone. We must allow ourselves to become the *objects* of Amida's practice without having recourse to our own misguided gropings which are destitute of any real vision.

"When the time comes
For shinjin, indestructible as diamond, to become settled,
Amida grasps and protects us with compassionate light,
So that we part forever from birth-and-death."

How are we transformed?

Much mention has already been made regarding the change that takes place when we enter into communion with Amida and are transfigured by the Primal Vow. But what does this mean in a practical sense and how do we benefit from it?

In our lives, we often find ourselves thrashed around by our reactions to the world, other people and our own state of mind. Sometimes we are uplifted by what affects us although, more often than not, we feel dejected or even threatened. This can give the impression that we are at the mercy of external forces we cannot control.

The reason why we become so rattled by life's events is that we identify ourselves with the unsteady mechanism of our minds and bodies; in other words, our everyday personality. We also have a strong tendency to depend on the world emotionally which, if unchecked, will invariably lead to lingering disenchantment when that reliance proves to be hollow in the long run.

In such cases, we tend to view any blows that we suffer from others or the world as harm done to who we really are. This can then lead to an all-consuming sense of resentful vulnerability. Buddhism's response to this problem is to throw down the challenge of questioning what we really take ourselves to be.

Shinran stated that our true self is Buddha-nature, not the confused clutter of feelings, memories and desires that we so ardently cling to as phenomena that define us. As discussed earlier, these are not the real bedrock of our existence. Even so, this reality remains present to us despite it being veiled in the layers of our quivering personality.

We can get a glimpse of our real essence, even in the midst of ordinary life, when we awaken to shinjin—the unfaltering mind of Amida that fills us with great joy and inexhaustible truth.

While this awakening will eventually lead to the attainment of Nirvana when our provisional personality dissolves at death, the unimaginable bliss of our final state cannot be fully experienced in this life given the many barriers we face in being creatures of 'blind passion' as Shinran described us.

Nevertheless, shinjin—as the vitalising presence in us of this immeasurable life—becomes a firm anchor in the rough ocean of samsara. When Amida reveals that which is 'true and real', we no longer feel driven to seek refuge in what is false and fleeting.

This means that the working of the Primal Vow provokes a shift at the centre of our being such that we find our identity firmly ensconced in eternal reality rather than in what only causes us worry, grief and dissatisfaction.

When we seek rest in this haven of light, our personality undergoes a renewal. We become subject to a radically different influence that gives strength, comfort and resilience in the face of life's repeatedly changing fortunes. This becomes possible because we find ourselves established in a reality that is compassionate and changeless, unlike anything we find in the world.

As a result, we remain the same regardless of what befalls us. Of course, we may feel crestfallen or disappointed when things go badly but, by securely dwelling in what we really are, we become sheltered by that which is imperishable and thus our true identity does not fluctuate. In this way, we can never be completely overwhelmed or defeated by the troubling vagaries of human existence.

Without this connection to what is immutable, any kind of worthwhile certainty will elude us and our quest for a sacred goal in life becomes fruitless. In this condition, we are not really living at all and our desperate attempts to make our lives seem fulfilled and relevant are no more effective than frantically slapping make-up on a corpse.

The other significant transformation that follows from the realisation of our true self is that we no longer bank on the world to give us unassailable happiness. Neither do we rely on ourselves to somehow generate an untroubled mind. The fact is that, when separated from the real life that is Amida, we're in a truly sorry state—despite how we may appear to be in the eyes of the world—because nothing in samsara can appease us for very long.

One of the names for Amida in the Shin Buddhist tradition is 'Light of Joy'. It is this joy that is given to us when we take refuge in that light which never ceases to shine in our hearts, whether we are aware of it or not. Because this joy flows from an eternal wellspring, it is always there to console us, particularly in difficult times.

Of course, we may not always feel this joy given our wayward and distracted natures. Yet Shinran reassures us by observing that, while our emotional response may undoubtedly vacillate from time to time, our faith still remains constant because it is rooted in the diamond-like nature of Amida's mind which is unbreakable. In other words, the knowledge of where deep tranquility can be found here and now will, without fail, bring us back to the bosom of this nurturing Light and Life.

The rejoicing imparted by this spiritual gift cannot be granted by the world. What we normally think of as happiness is simply too precarious and insecure, no matter how delectable it feels at the time. A well-being that is genuine must not be based on such shaky foundations.

It should be a little clearer now in what sense we can be transformed by the action of Amida's forceful effect on us. The Primal Vow that wills the deliverance of all beings actively seeks them out, compassionately calling on us to submit our lost and wounded hearts to its warming embrace.

When this happens, we feel emboldened by an unwavering trust and find rest from the turmoil of our lives as the unhindered light of Amida scatters the shadows of this dream-like existence so that we may finally wake up.

Nothing can exceed a joy such as this and nothing can take it away. We are urged to give up the dead weight of our innumerable problems to the working of Amida who will then transform us from 'bits of rubble into gold' as Shinran remarks.

When we do this, serenity descends into our hearts and the suffering associated with our tribulations is lifted from us because we come to know that there is something greater that forever sustains our lives.

How are we transformed?

So, when it comes to what is of real spiritual value, we can now see—beyond any doubt—that *everything is given to us.*

"When the waters of the mind entrusting to Other-Power enter
The ocean waters of Amida's Vow of wisdom,
Then, in accord with the nature of the Pure Land,
Blind passions and enlightenment come to be of one taste."

What about my imperfections?

Many of those who sincerely attempt to live a spiritual life, quickly come to confront the sobering reality of their own fallibility. If some kind of perfection is demanded of them, they will inevitably become despondent at their lack of progress.

When faced with these set-backs, people are encouraged to practise harder but, when there is no improvement, they lose heart and end up being lukewarm in their commitment. If the discouragement is serious enough, spiritual discipline can be abandoned altogether.

Some say that what only matters is the effort to never give up and become the best we can, regardless of results. So we persist with our meditation (even when it feels dry and empty) or our attempts at good works (even though we are always stumbling).

We wonder, as mentioned earlier, how much practice is enough to know that we're making progress; if a loss of confidence sets in, we will reluctantly go back to pursuits where the rewards, even though short-lived, appear more tangible and immediate.

Shinran was keenly aware of the challenges faced by practitioners but what distinguished his approach was the honesty with which he tackled the problem at its source. He simply had to face the pitfalls of our tenuous nature that prevented him from overcoming his weaknesses and attaining perfect enlightenment in this life. This went against the grain of the established Buddhist schools of that period and led to much persecution, eventually resulting in his exile.

The hindrance posed by our passions was clearly acknowledged by Shinran during his time as a monk. Even though he was considered very conscientious, he honestly admitted to having failed in his monastic discipline. Problems with distracted concentration and the temptation of binding desires made him see the futility (and paradox) of trying to crush his limitations through practices that were, in themselves, subject to the very same limitations.

The spiritual crisis that followed prompted him to seek out Honen, who would become his master. This fateful encounter completely changed his view on the human condition, which led him to reconsider what real practice was and how we could benefit from it.

Shinran never gave up on fulfilling the aims of Buddhist life so, of course, he continued to believe in the goal of attaining wisdom and, ultimately, Nirvana. It's just that he became convinced that the practices we undertake are of no avail in light of the powerful constraints that frequently paralyse us. As we are simply lost unenlightened beings, we can only be tossed about helplessly by the violent waves of greed, lust, ill will and ignorance.

Because he couldn't see how we—being inherently deficient—can possibly perfect ourselves, Shinran realised that some kind of radical intervention is necessary. This cannot be of human origin because even the most exalted masters are still mortal beings who can only but point the way to the sole resolution of this dilemma.

So, if we're unable to surmount our failings, where does that leave our practice? After we've exhausted all efforts to improve ourselves, we come to see that the ego simply cannot cure itself. Trying to do this is like rearranging the deck chairs on the Titanic as it is sinking—nothing really changes and the end is inevitable.

The startling conclusion reached by Shinran is that our numerous personal failings are not a handicap in meeting our spiritual aspirations because the true font of liberation is the Other-Power of Amida—the active dimension of this inconceivable ultimate reality.

Our inadequacies are a natural consequence of being limited beings, which means we often get confused, lash out in anger, behave cruelly or do stupid things when prompted by our fierce drives and aversions. Given that this is our sad reality, how could we ever depend on such a damaged self to rescue us from what the Buddha described as the 'burning house' that is our hazardous existence in this world?

Yes, by all means avoid harming others wherever you can but are we always so sure in what harm consists? An ostensible improvement in one sphere of life can lead to intractable problems in another. We are not omniscient and the facts of any given (and often unimaginably complex) situation are not always clear to us.

Of course, we should aim to follow a wholesome life in accordance with the Buddha's teachings as this doubtlessly helps to improve our lives (even though we regrettably often fail to do so). However, unless we turn for refuge in the pure light that is Amida, no effective spiritual transformation can ever take place.

The weaknesses with which we're weighed down in life at least have the advantage of helping us develop an attitude of humility and self-awareness. This inclines us to be more empathetic towards others as we come to realise that they too suffer from the same frailties. Reflecting on ourselves in this way also curbs our strong tendency to be judgemental, sanctimonious and hypocritical.

We can see ourselves for what we truly are—painful as this is—only in the light of Amida's piercing wisdom. This is real self-knowledge that spurs us to take refuge so that we don't have to count on our ineffectual efforts to tame the pernicious 'snakes and scorpions' of our minds.

Sooner or later, we must face the uncomfortable truth that conventional self-generated spiritual practices have failed to perfect us and that we often remain profoundly foolish and limited beings. We can only become awakened to this fact in light of a greater, all-inclusive reality that illumines our condition and, despite our shortcomings, shows us a better way to be.

This is in keeping with Shinran's assessment of ordinary beings and their failure to scrupulously observe the requirements of the Buddha's stern injunctions during a time when human nature has become thoroughly decadent.

A life informed by wisdom and compassion cannot be compelled but must reflect the unforced impact of this reality in our lives. Therefore, our primary objective is spiritual transformation while remaining fully conscious of being encumbered by our disfigured humanity.

We only compound these infirmities by perpetuating a life absorbed by the three poisons of greed, hatred and ignorance; such an existence cannot overcome its own illness. Without a firm footing in the ultimate reality that Buddhism implores us to rely on, we are bound to continue our tragic and aimless vagrancy in further rounds of transmigration, regardless of how healthy, comfortable or affluent we may be.

If we can deliver up to Amida the personal baggage that prevents us from flourishing spiritually, the compassionate sway of the Primal Vow will bring about the remarkable effect of making us 'soft and gentle in body and mind' as the Buddhist scriptures observe.

Shinran speaks of the transformation that takes place when we are enfolded by the majestic virtues of Amida's light whereby the "ice of our blind passions necessarily melts, becoming the water of enlightenment." He goes on to say that the "obstruction of our karmic afflictions turn into virtues; it is like the relation of ice and water; the more ice, the more water; the more obstructions, the more virtues."

In this way, we are given to understand that these passions, which can be so heated, are able to be turned into spiritual virtues that are given to us when we relinquish, with great relief, our imperfections to the workings of the Primal Vow. The suffering they cause is then alleviated because the darkness of these afflictions—which previously divided us from Amida's light—is dispersed in the joy of being grasped by true compassion, never to be abandoned.

"Because the power of the Vow is without limits,
Even our karma, so deep and heavy is not burdensome; because the
Buddha's wisdom is without bounds, even the bewildered and wayward
are not abandoned ... Since we are possessed of blind passions, the Bud-
dha receives us without judging whether our hearts are good or bad."

How do we entrust?

We don't have to look far today to see despairing people all around us. We despair about our health, careers, relationships, society, our families, the environment and so on. Essentially, this reflects a fundamental unease about ourselves.

We grapple with our worries and doubts as we look to find solutions to a problem that doesn't seem to go away. Aiming to project a strong and confident sense of self to the world, we merely end up becoming a burden to ourselves.

Keeping up appearances is a struggle because, deep down, we often see that much of what we present to others is a sham. We want to be liked, respected and admired when we very often do not, in all honesty, feel that way about ourselves.

But because the fear of death is so great—even among those who pretend to deny it—we develop what the Buddha called the 'craving to be'; a striving to maintain a distinct personality with which we identify in order to keep at bay our terror of annihilation.

Even if we can admit to ourselves that we're not all that wonderful, we still feel that any kind of existence, however unsatisfactory, is far preferable to the oblivion of our mortality. If we believe that this is all there is—that our precious personality is the only reality possible for us—then we'll aim to preserve it at all costs. Truth, justice and the interests of others are then readily sacrificed to ensure the integrity of 'myself' and its needs.

Of course, we are all aware of rare souls who resist this tendency and sometimes give up their very lives for something greater than themselves but this suggests, precisely, that our own narrow existence is not always the supreme value in life.

The Buddha taught that there is an alternative to non-existence, as we understand it, and that awakening to it is the only real solution to the problems that oppress us. Left to our own devices, we just keep going around and around in a lifeless repetitive cycle of ego affirmation which leaves us unfulfilled because there is no joy or freedom in it.

The fractures in our hearts can, indeed, be harrowing but they may also let in the healing light if we allow it to do so. This boundless wisdom that is disclosed in our lives relentlessly seeks to unbind us from our spurious sense of self and the desolation it brings.

It is important to understand here that we are not talking about some kind of remote deity that is separate from the world with unpredictable character traits, not unlike our own in fact. By contrast, the Buddha revealed that Amida is the unfailingly benign face assumed by this omnipresent life in order to become known to beings like us who need a living connection with a reality that is accessible, seeing as we are restricted to time and space.

As discussed earlier, the real self is not our mundane personality. It is neither the body, the functions of the mind, nor the peculiarities of our character—indeed, consciousness is even more fluctuating than our bodies. Our true form, on the other hand, is not subject to change and, as such, does not suffer.

We can see, therefore, that we are sparks or embodiments of this ultimate reality. That's why we can go back to it—because there is something of it in us—and the way to return is through what Shinran calls *shinjin*. This is sometimes translated as 'entrusting heart' or 'endowed trust' (because it is given rather than earned) but it's also the vehicle that allows us to know spiritual reality *directly* as a living fact to be appreciated.

In other words, it is a faculty of intuitive knowledge (not a mere idea or dogmatic belief in something) that constitutes its own proof or validation. It is what enables us to see that our lives are caught up in shifting appearances and how we've become lost in a world that often feels meaningless. We cannot perceive this truth by simply relying on the ego. We are *made* to see this through the revealing light of wisdom which is the working of Other-Power.

So how do we entrust? Shinjin is an attitude of complete reliance on the Primal Vow, which is the compassionate resolve of Amida that works to free us from the slavery of our dark minds. It means letting go of self-working which believes that, through our ailing efforts, we are somehow able to vanquish our unhappiness and disquiet. More importantly, it also entails giving up the suffering caused by our emotional responses to others and the world.

Seeing as we're unable to remedy the maladies of existence, we can only surrender all that we are to Amida's working which has the effect of gradually relieving our anguish. The weight of our harmful desires is then lifted, thereby freeing us from the onerous expectation of having to lean on ourselves alone.

We simply hand over to Amida all those thoughts and feelings that cause us vexation and let Other-Power shine on them, like sunlight that purifies and disinfects. When we do so, we feel a quiet and gentle joy that comes with knowing that we're thoroughly accepted as we are, in all our fretful inconstancy. Regardless of how messed up our lives get, this limitless compassion never judges or rejects us.

Because we are not depending on our own strength, virtue or wisdom, it doesn't matter that we are helpless and troubled beings. Amida full well knows our dismal condition and willingly extends a saving hand to pull us out of our private hells.

Of course, we will very often stray from this entrusting because we continue to be fallibly human but that is not important. We are constantly summoned back and, when we heed that call, are prompted to return swiftly to a refuge that is secure and restful; only then can we be truly at peace with ourselves.

Nothing is asked of us except our consent for this to happen. We are not expected to contribute anything other than our harassing desires and an admission of our inability to deal with them. There is no requirement here for any kind of moral perfection or the ability to thoroughly conquer all our weaknesses.

Because we find ourselves entrenched in something deeper and more stable than the 'snakes and scorpions' of our minds or the 'burning house' of this world, our anxious burdens are transformed into a calm acceptance of how things really are. This brings us to know that we cannot be harmed by the transient forces of this life and that our eternal spiritual destiny is secure.

Many fear that this simply leaves us with nothing but that is not so.

How do we entrust?

The effect of such a realisation is that *we* (<u>not</u> our minds or emotions) become quiet because our serene Buddha-nature then emerges as the real basis of our abiding universal personhood (as opposed to our ever-changing ordinary self).

With the emergence of shinjin, we recognise ourselves—even more vividly—as hurting, lost and confused. At the same time, we are also uplifted with an awareness animated by that which is 'true and real'. Both these insights arise together as a result of Amida's influence on us.

This inevitably confers a deep sense of respite that comes with savouring the compassionate activity of Other-Power, even in the midst of our hectic routines. In this way, the blooming of shinjin enables the joyous qualities of Amida to become active in our otherwise flustered lives.

Experiencing nothing but dejection is extremely difficult to endure and would only make us want to live in complete denial about our woeful condition. But when such a grave awareness is accompanied by the very solution needed to free us from that predicament, our trepidation is converted into a lasting composure that this uncertain world can never threaten.

"Entrusting is the mind full of truth, reality and sincerity; the mind of ultimacy, accomplishment, reliance and reverence; the mind of discernment, distinctness, clarity and faithfulness; the mind of aspiration and exultation; the mind of delight, joy, gladness and happiness; hence, it is completely untainted by the hindrance of doubt . . . Although they neither seek nor know the indescribable, inexplicable, and inconceivable virtues of the Pure Land of happiness, those who entrust themselves to the Primal Vow are made to acquire them."

Can I ever become a better person?

The teaching of the Shin Buddhist tradition insists that we are not Buddhas and can never become so in this life. Being incomplete is a fundamental aspect of our human condition. Despite our best endeavours, we find—as Shinran forcefully reminds us—that "our desires are countless, and anger, wrath, jealousy and envy are overwhelming, arising without pause; to the very last moment of life they do not cease, disappear or exhaust themselves".

So if becoming a better person means eliminating these features from our lives, then we can never attain such a goal. This is impossible, even for the most generous and kind-hearted person. These comprise fundamental aspects to who we are that can't entirely be eradicated although they can be turned into something spiritually fruitful.

An important consideration here is to recognise that we are not responsible for the torrent of thoughts that enter our minds. Shinran is very clear that our karmic history throws up all manner of strange, disturbing and troublesome notions that can prove very unsettling. All these have a cause and form part of the inheritance that we've brought into this life, which continues to develop in accordance with our character and environment.

This does not mean that we are, in any way, entitled to act out such thoughts in our lives; our moral responsibility definitely kicks in when we give effect to impulses that are harmful to others and ourselves. It may well be that we do sometimes lose control and pursue desires that are damaging even though appearing to be uncalculated or impulsive. Even so, we are called to account for such behaviour and must wear the consequences in this life, either in terms of punishment by the law, social humiliation or karmic retribution.

While Shinran's view may seem severe in its realism, he actually offers much hope to those prepared to rely on the benevolent potency of Other-Power to melt the hard ice of our unruly desires into the undisturbed waters of quietude. Entrusting in this reality, instead of oneself, is not being 'lazy' or morally lax. It is simply recognising the very real limits we face when trying to improve ourselves through self-willed efforts.

In one of his letters, Shinran says: "Formerly you were drunk with the wine of ignorance and had a liking only for the three poisons of greed, anger and folly but, since you have begun to hear of the Buddha's Vow, you have awakened from the drunkenness of ignorance, gradually rejected the three poisons and have come to prefer, at all times, the medicine of Amida Buddha."

This clearly suggests that our behaviour can be modified through an acquiescent and unresisting exposure to the unbounded Light and Life at the heart of existence. We don't have to do anything other than listen for that quiet voice that calls and to let it do its work.

No special virtue is required of us but when we are wholeheartedly receptive in this way over a period of time, "surely there are signs of rejecting the evil of this world and a desire to cast off the evil in ourselves" as Shinran's letter concludes.

What he means by 'evil' here is not just moral wickedness as many understand it (which of course doesn't apply to most people). Rather, it's a penetrating admission of the ego's inability—when bereft of Amida's purifying light—to rise above its selfish promptings or perform any genuinely good acts.

Needless to say, all this has nothing to do with the self-improvement of character based on an idealistic notion of moral perfection which, when thwarted, can only lead to frustration and even self-loathing. Instead, by responding to the working of the Primal Vow, we experience a shift at the core of our being such that we are no longer *governed* by our mercurial impulses even though we may still suffer from some of their effects.

In that sense, a disposition towards moral behaviour emerges as a natural consequence of this awareness and is not something we exhibit for the sake of earning merit or 'salvation'.

Shinran also observes that "When people's trust in the Buddha has grown deep, they come to abhor such a self and to lament their continued existence in birth-and-death; such a person then joyfully says the name of Amida deeply entrusting themselves to the Vow. That people seek to stop doing wrong as the heart moves them—although earlier they gave thought to such things and committed them as their minds dictated—is surely a sign of having rejected this world."

What this means is that the light of Amida prompts us towards becoming spiritually mature beings who are able to show kindness, care and concern for others. We are made to conform, as much as possible within our human constraints, to the moral order of the cosmos which is something objective and embedded in the very nature of ultimate reality.

Unless this reality comes alive in us, we can only continue to circle confusedly in what seems like a dark empty room where we find ourselves full of miserable agitation. We obsess about the past and fret about our future while failing to live fully in the present—the only place in which this unceasing wisdom and compassion can become real for us.

No doubt we will flounder as we aim to remain faithful to this vision of goodness, truth and beauty that charges our lives with meaning but we are never condemned when we don't succeed. Amida is pure unconditional compassion and enfolds all beings with tenderness regardless of our failures. These are of no concern to Amida whose only desire is to save us from our swollen self-absorption.

Some might object that this teaching actually undermines our confidence and sense of personal worth, which many consider very important today. Yet Buddhism has no interest in developing our 'self-esteem' which it sees as the underlying cause of our conceited arrogance and pride.

Having a perfectly normal and healthy regard for oneself, on the other hand, is very important so that we don't neglect our worldly interests or the responsibilities we have to others but this attitude must, at all times, be informed by an unpretentious self-awareness.

And so, we should not deprecate or condemn ourselves unjustly seeing as the Buddha clearly opposed all forms of hatred including towards oneself. The point, rather, is to form a completely honest and impartial view of who we are even if it may be distasteful or confronting.

Truth must always prevail over our emotional reactions to the facts of existence. Such responses are informed by fear and vanity which have nothing to do with living authentically. But when rightly directed towards a spiritual object, our emotions can play a decisive role in lifting us out of our confused subjectivity as suggested by the Latin origin of the word (*emovere*) which means to 'move out'. Thinking alone cannot achieve this seeing as the heart, as the seat of our emotions, must also be involved.

Genuine humility is only possible when we are grounded in true reality. It alone can show us the unvarnished truth regarding our real plight in this doleful realm of birth and death. When we become fully aware of—not just the tenacious obstacles that keeps us firmly trapped in self-deception—but the beneficent help available to us through the working of the Primal Vow, we cease to judge both others and ourselves.

We are then left only with receiving the transforming grace given to us through our entrusting hearts as conferred by Amida.

So to answer our original question, yes we can become better people but not through any virtue that we're able to summon from our wounded selves. In the end, compassionate and ethical behaviour can only be a consequence, not a condition, of spiritual awakening.

When we are cut off from Amida's Life—which is like a cool refreshing breeze—we continue to remain ensnared by the blistering assault of our fierce yet futile infatuations.

There can never be any improvement in ourselves under such irredeemable conditions. Our only solution is to heed the call urging us to take unshaken refuge in that which is abidingly free of all doubt and consternation.

———————————

"Do not meaninglessly despise yourself, weaken your heart, and doubt the Buddha's wisdom, which surpasses conceptual understanding. . . . The mind of trust alone is essential. There is no need to consider anything else."

What does it mean to take refuge?

The taking of refuge goes back to the earliest days of Buddhism. During that time, it was considered vitally important to rely on the wisdom of the Buddha, the teachings he left behind and the community he founded.

As the Buddhist tradition developed over the centuries into what became the Mahayana (or 'Greater Vehicle'), the object of refuge continued to be the teachings and community of followers but the focus of devotion gradually shifted away from the historical Buddha, Shakyamuni.

This was because, after his death, disciples began to discern that what made him enlightened was a quality or presence transcending his earthly personality which could, nevertheless, continue to furnish spiritual guidance in this life.

In Shin Buddhism, this presence—known to us as *Amida*—is a dimension of ultimate reality that has taken form as a great cosmic Buddha which permeates, yet surpasses, all things. According to the tradition, it was this Buddha that Shakyamuni became awakened to in his enlightenment under the Bodhi Tree. Indeed, the time-bound Buddha of history is seen as a manifestation, in our world, of the limitless one in response to the needs of suffering beings.

For Shinran, it is Amida that is the true object of our refuge. As Shakyamuni is no longer among us as a living presence, we must be supported by the reality that lies behind his enlightenment; something that is ever-present to us now, with which we can have a relationship that is supremely intimate.

Having clarified the origins of this notion, how are we to understand the taking of refuge in a practical sense? What are we expected to do? The first thing one might ask is why we should even worry about refuge in the first place. Is there anything about our situation in life that makes it necessary?

We have previously mentioned the fact of our 'incompleteness' as human beings. When we reflect on ourselves, we sense an innate need for spiritual fullness. In ordinary life, we sometimes feel dislocated as if we're not entirely in tune with our surroundings. There is a sense of isolation in realising how remote we can be from others or, indeed, from any sources of significant meaning in our lives.

What constitutes human flourishing? Is it simply physical comfort and convenience? One could argue, for instance, that our great-grandparents led happier and more purposeful lives than us even though they lived under much more difficult conditions. Perhaps this had to do with greater resilience, wisdom and prudence or the quality of their relationships. In any case, the point is that we often mistake what we really need for things that are of no real benefit to us.

Shinran insisted that we must take refuge in that which is 'true and real', in contrast to what he called the 'lies and gibberish' of this world where so much unreality and falsehood abounds. Moreover, our minds and bodies also happen to be on fire with the flames of greed, lust, hatred and delusion. Therefore there is nothing in us, either, in which we can take refuge.

Our besieged self cannot offer anything capable of giving us equilibrium and stability in the face of life's vicissitudes. We often resist this difficult truth because we feel that it would mean somehow losing autonomy—the sense of being in control of our lives—which we take to be crucial to who we are. However, this independence that we value so much will seem as nothing when we are shown our complete reliance on the immense life that transcends us and sustains all things.

If we cannot bank on our body, intellect, feelings, opinions—or our personality generally—to withstand the onslaught of life's misfortunes, then we are in trouble. Unless, of course, we have found something that is more than just what happens to pass away. If we do discover this, then there is an end to the agonising ordeal involved in resisting all those forces that threaten our identity and sense of self-worth.

When confronted by that which is wholly trustworthy, we no longer fight back against our imagined foes and learn to accept the unchangeable realities of life. In doing so, the aggrieved ego is finally resolved in the light of Amida, accepts its limitations and finds peace.

After a while, we are made to see that it is not the external world that is the problem but, rather, our reaction to it. This means that we must be transformed by the workings of the Primal Vow so that we're able to remain largely undaunted in the face of life's changing circumstances which are, for the most part, beyond our powers to influence or control.

The value of life should not wholly depend on external occurrences or on anything that can be taken away from us. We see this attitude exemplified in the following remark by Shinran: "Although my defiled life is filled with all kinds of desires and delusions, my mind is playing in the Pure Land".

The word *refuge* means to seek shelter or protection from a place of danger or difficulty. It derives from the Latin *re-fugere*, to 'flee back' to something. The wisdom imparted by Amida reveals that nothing in this world can completely fulfill our desires, such that desire is forever eliminated. This is because our hearts are made for something that vastly exceeds this world.

In other words, our true refuge must be in that which puts an end to not only old age, sickness and death but also the torments of human love, sorrow and pleasure; that is, we are encouraged to seek safe harbour in a happiness that can never be lost.

In tackling the practical question of how we take refuge, Shinran encourages us to discard the mind of self-power by not trying "to make yourself worthy through mending the confusion in your acts, words and thoughts, confident of your own powers and guided by your own calculation".

He also admonishes us to "abandon the conviction that one is good, to cease relying on the self; to stop reflecting knowingly on one's evil heart and, further, to abandon the judging of people as good and bad".

When this happens, we notice a gradual conversion in us whereby we come to rest in what feels like a secure clasp that will not let us go.

What does it mean to take refuge?

This isn't just some sentimental illusion in desperate response to our need for comfort in the face of an uncertain future—a common criticism of religion today.

On the contrary, we are presented here with something very real that can be verified through the impact it has on our lives. The working of the Primal Vow envelops us in a vivid awareness that is gentle and composed.

Seeing as we clearly do not possess such qualities ourselves, we're able to understand that they are not something we have created from the poor ingredients of our blighted personalities. In this way, we come to acquire a natural and unforced humility. Also, when we find ourselves at ease in this embrace, our suffering is lightened because we discover our true self that is invulnerable.

This is what the tradition means by spiritual protection, regardless of what happens to our bodies. Resting in Amida's Light and Life *is* freedom; therefore we feel truly at home in it and come to reject the preoccupations of our little self and its tyrannical obsessions.

As the world cannot give us this composure, neither can it deprive us of it; and while our ailing human nature still remains intact, its potential to disturb us is subdued, like a scorpion deprived of its sting.

To take refuge in Amida is simply to discard everything about us that is not reliable. This, of course, does not mean neglecting our duties and responsibilities in life but it does imply that we don't confuse functional living with the authentic life that is only possible when Amida's mind arises and becomes settled in us. Shinran describes it as indestructible, like a diamond, in contrast to our own unstable thoughts and feelings.

The vow that Amida made to rescue all beings from their terrible plight is also an encouragement to seek the help that is always available to us. To accept it with thankfulness is not some kind of weak capitulation or a simple concession to fear. It is the dawning of wisdom in us that sees the need for there to be less of 'us' and more of Amida in our hearts and minds.

Taking refuge is to receive the warming light so that our chilly dark-ness is banished. This is dying to our false self—the origin of all grief—and becoming rejuvenated as a being destined for Nirvana, a foretaste of which is given to us even now as we rejoice in the great message of unconditional compassion that declares: "No one is left behind".

"When we come to know truly that we are possessed of blind passions,
And entrust ourselves to the power of the Primal Vow,
We will, on abandoning completely our defiled existence,
Realise the eternal bliss of dharma-nature."

Conclusion: A Synopsis
of Shin Buddhism

It may be useful now to consider how the foregoing reflections relate to some major themes in Shin Buddhism. While it is profitable to understand its teachings by the direct impression they make on our lives in a practical sense, we must also remember that there is a living historical tradition that has sustained these insights over many centuries.

We have already touched on some of the key notions that are central to Shinran's vision but it might also be helpful to provide a wide-ranging overview of how they hang together to form a coherent whole, even though the following observations may not be entirely systematic in their sequence.

The 21st century has clearly made remarkable technological advances—and this to an extraordinary degree—but our era can hardly be considered wise. Its affluence often distracts us from the harsh realities of sickness, ageing and death which we're always trying to avert or control. But the Buddha clearly warned us of the futility of ever overcoming these misfortunes altogether.

Instead, we look for false alleviation from our anxiety precisely through such things as the comforts and convenience of technology—to the extent that certain advocates of artificial intelligence confidently predict that they will even find the key to ensuring our earthly immortality (if such a thing could ever be truly desirable).

In the end, though, our means of securing freedom from angst lie elsewhere—beyond the crushing boredom, heartless narcissism and withering numbness prevalent in so much of modern life where, having become dead on the inside, we find ourselves lacking in genuine convictions because we believe everything to be only relative or subjective and thus reducible to what is merely natural.

This is part and parcel of a growing secularisation that we are witnessing today along with the gradual stripping away of any spiritual dimension to our lives. In other words, we are slowly losing a sense of the sacred.

As indicated earlier, the Buddha described our world as a 'burning house' of transience where no true sanctuary can be found. Our lives, which are studded with so many uncertainties, often feel defenceless. We also find ourselves driven by unease and the need for self-preservation at all costs.

Much of modern life is limited to the satisfaction of either our physical imperatives or our vanity. Even if these were completely achievable (which is most unlikely), what happens next? We are still the same confused beings we were before, struggling to find fulfillment and happiness in this unsettled realm of birth-and-death.

A major crisis in our world today is the absence of meaning, a lost awareness of the transcendent and a corresponding degradation of our dignity as beings who need to fulfill their true vocation as wayfarers on a journey back to our source. Shin Buddhism offers a definitive response to these challenges by inviting us to rediscover and assert our spiritual nobility in seeking the deepest truths, despite our human frailties.

The rise of this tradition was in response to a number of factors, during the time of Shinran, that weighed heavily on his followers. Firstly, there was the need to make Nirvana more accessible to ordinary folk through the use of rich and positive symbolism designed to heighten their aspiration for it. Secondly, we see a clear recognition of the difficulty in attaining full enlightenment in the present life during what is considered an age when the efficacy of mainstream Buddhist practices has become largely corrupted.

Perhaps more than any other Buddhist tradition, Shinran's convictions have been the most sensitive to the needs of sincere individuals who are battling with personal weakness and the seemingly insurmountable barriers of anger, greed and ignorance.

We hear much about enlightenment but how should we understand it? Essentially, it can only mean the elimination of every aspect of our ordinary self that separates us from the supreme reality, in the face of which our lives must appear as so many fragile bubbles lacking any inherent substance.

Given the persistent difficulties and paradoxes of our life in this world, Shinran's insights offer hope to those for whom perfection seems utterly elusive. It does so through the assurance of spiritual release via the workings of the Primal Vow which is manifested in us through our saying of Amida's Name.

This is why the tradition calls this activity 'Other-Power' (*tariki*); because, as the basis of all spiritual endeavour, it transcends the stifling confines of the ego. It is also the capacity of Amida to shield us from our perilous condition, which neutralises any dependence on our own spiritual impotence. In fact, Other-Power is the only real power that exists because it is the force behind the only reality there is.

It is important to understand that Shinran did not deny that we could spiritually improve ourselves through ethical cultivation and meditation, at least in principle. He respected what he called the 'Path of Sages' which was largely a monastic way of life that relied on personal effort and initiative. It's just that he considered this path out of reach for the great mass of humanity given the reality of its debilitated condition.

Shinran's teaching is particularly suited to the capacities of people in our time. This accounts for its great reach and popularity over the course of its history—and for the fact that shinjin, as our final end in this life, can be attained in the midst of toilsome everyday existence. As a result, our moral lives can also improve but naturally and without contrivance.

This gives it a vitality that can inspire those who seek refuge in it because it engages us in precisely the condition in which we find ourselves. It does not ask for the impossible, though this path is not without its own difficulties.

The question is often asked as to what will happen to wicked or vicious people when they die—does Amida ignore their deeds and save them regardless? It is the absolute desire of Amida to emancipate all beings but they must want to be saved and this presupposes contrition for one's harmful acts. Until they admit this undying life into their hearts, karma that is generated with a mind of delusion will continue to propel them into uncertain destinies.

As all karma is finite, it will eventually exhaust itself but this may take much longer for some than others, depending on its severity. Amida will finally break through and reverse the adverse karmic currents of everyone because even grossly ignorant or depraved beings cannot resist indefinitely.

And, yes, even the likes of Stalin, Hitler, Mao and Pol Pot are embraced by Amida and destined for Nirvana; but only after having been through a complete transformation following exposure to hellish conditions (which can never be eternal) where their defilements will undergo extensive purging to eventually unveil the Buddhanature within.

But what about someone who supposedly has 'faith' in Amida but behaves abominably? Do they get a 'free pass' to the Pure Land? I believe Shinran would say that a person of real shinjin, while faltering many times in their moral life, would never be capable of any truly heinous crimes.

In certain cases, though, such an individual's karma may be so detrimental that it can sometimes, albeit briefly, overwhelm their free will during intense episodes of vehement passion, leading to actions that are quickly regretted and the subject of very great remorse.

Shin Buddhism has sometimes been called 'do-nothing Buddhism' because its followers do not practice in order to amend their faults and improve themselves through meditative practices or good deeds.

The radical nature of this teaching can seem quite extreme or confronting, as it was even among Shinran's contemporaries. One hopes that enough has been said during the course of this study to show that it simply isn't true that one does nothing. Given the subtlety of Shinran's approach, it does not easily conform to a commonplace understanding of practice, as one would expect from an Other-Power perspective.

What makes Shin Buddhism challenging is that it involves, among other things, a reflection on the nature of the Primal Vow as the basis for true practice. In doing so, it removes any possibility that entrusting or taking refuge, while undoubtedly being something that *we* do, is a virtue that can ever be claimed as our own.

Nembutsu, the practice of hearing and saying Amida's Name (*Namu Amida Butsu* in Japanese) as a contemplative act arising from Other-Power, opens us up to the universal influence of ultimate reality which undertakes true practice on our behalf. We must therefore make room for its working in our hearts and minds. This is the only spiritually beneficial act of which we are capable.

This may suggest an attitude that is rather passive but—despite appearances—it is far from being idle. It entails a life of constant engagement with the teachings and, through them, exposure to the wisdom of Amida.

So what often commences as a struggle comes, over time, to be bathed in the reality of the Primal Vow, so that every self-effort is finally renounced in light of the Vow's exposure of our shortcomings. This is what represents the unique value of the nembutsu—it completely unmasks our nature as ordinary people (*bombu*) while, at the same time, foreshadowing the joy of our spiritual deliverance.

As we have already seen, shinjin is radiant Buddha-nature that becomes disclosed to us as our true self, which can only be revealed by the action of Other–Power. This decisive encounter with the real living presence of Amida is a consoling oasis in the midst of our restless lives which we express, with effortless praise, in our saying of the nembutsu. This evokes a powerful intuition that sharply perceives the way things are, unlike reason which can only draw conclusions based on what is provided from sources outside itself.

Shinjin, then, is an immediate way of knowing spiritual reality, without which we would be unable to perceive anything other than just physical and mental phenomena. This insight challenges the mistaken belief that our existence is restricted solely to the natural world and that we can't establish any certain truths beyond what the scientific method is able to reveal to us. In this way, we are invited to adopt an altogether different and more thorough understanding of reality.

It is usually hardness of heart that precludes this vision; and notice we say 'heart' rather than 'mind' in order to stress that what is at fault here is a spiritual rather than a mere intellectual blindness. Shinjin, then, connects us to what is real—hence it is rightly considered a form of realisation or awakening.

But how does this differ from a 'religious experience'? The latter suggests a passing event, albeit life-changing, whereas shinjin is an ongoing awareness of Amida as an all-permeating presence in our lives.

To have shinjin is to come into contact with spiritual truth and, in this respect, it is also religious in nature but not in the sense of being strictly bound by any formal doctrinal limits. It is a vision that exceeds worldly understanding but which infuses our habitual lives with wonder and reverence towards the inconceivable.

This is what must be restored and cherished if we are to maintain a fulfilling inner life. There is no substitute for doing so and we must strive to awaken it in both ourselves and others.

Shin Buddhism is available to everyone without exception. It imposes no requirements on us other than a deep commitment to seek the truth and be freed from our suffering, along with a willingness to take the 'medicine' dispensed by Amida Buddha. This is done by casting ourselves onto the workings of the Primal Vow through steady reflection arising from 'deep hearing' (*monpo*).

In receiving and accepting an invitation to entrust, we patiently await the breakthrough of the light, just as we might eagerly expect the arrival of dawn. We cannot compel its appearance or force ourselves onto it. Amida's presence imbues our life, regardless of what's happening around us, because all existence is immersed in its unlimited resplendence.

In Mahayana Buddhism, the notion of Nirvana developed further such that it became invested—not only with the attributes of wisdom and blissful liberation—but active compassion as well; a reaching out to suffering beings that are only so many aspects of itself, which is what accounts for the indissoluble bond between Amida and ourselves.

The Mahayana openly acknowledges the existence of a supreme reality that, as we have seen, is not only known as Nirvana (being the state of complete freedom from ignorance and suffering) but also the Dharma-Body considered as the Absolute.

The Dharma-Body lies beyond anything we can perceive or apprehend. Even so, it dwells in all things which is what allows us to know it directly, in that we become aware of its existence through that part of us which shares in its nature.

According to the Mahayana, the world is a spontaneous expression of the Dharma-Body—there is no conscious design or willed creation out of nothing as we find in theistic religions. This manifestation is an endlessly cyclical process that does not have a discernible origin in time. Samsara is thus also dependent for its reality on the Dharma-Body although the particulars of its genesis cannot be determined.

It is as though this reality affirms itself in a manner that is incomplete while remaining inseparable from its own infinite essence. The Dharma-Body, as a consequence of its limitless nature and the dictates of karmic necessity, adopts countless finite forms through which it expresses itself as the world.

Furthermore, as already mentioned, the Dharma-Body is not omnipotent (as God must be in some religions). After all, a major stumbling block for theistic faith is the difficulty of reconciling the goodness and purported omnipotence of God with the incomprehensible misery we find in the world. In fact, one might well argue that it is quite impossible to do so.

Buddhism offers the distinct advantage of not positing an all-powerful deity that brings creation into being through a conscious act of will. And yet, in the non-dual vision of the Mahayana, the supreme bliss of Nirvana is not remote from the ordeals of this life but neither are they identical. To be sure, this is a profound yet unavoidable mystery at the very heart of reality.

The conditions of samsara cannot be other than what they are seeing as the impersonal law of karma reigns supreme in our world, dispensing its justice without favour or partiality.

While we can certainly remain fearful of our karma and what it may have in store for us, our response to Amida can only be one of love and adoration. Amida—who only desires to unchain us from these bonds—never seeks to 'punish' anyone for their transgressions. Only karma can do that.

Without the intervention of Amida's light in our life to steer us towards the Pure Land of Nirvana, the moral order of the cosmos will simply deliver the appropriate consequences of breaching karmic laws, leading to ongoing transmigration.

What this means is that, in this very life, we can begin putting an end to our melancholy odyssey. Take, for example, a plant that is plucked out of its soil—there is still some nourishment in its roots and the plant is able to survive for just a while longer even though it is wilting.

Similarly, without violating the law of cause and effect, Amida disrupts the future consequences of our karma by pulling our ailing roots out of the dirt of samsara. The negative energy that has fuelled our transmigration for countless lives is then forever cut off. Even though we continue to live on for a short time after that, there is no more nutrition left to feed our counterfeit self. Therefore, when we die, we become completely liberated from karmic bondage.

By virtue of its very nature, samsara is disordered and deficient—it can never become an earthly paradise for it does not possess the qualities of Nirvana; namely eternity, bliss and purity which are reserved solely for that which is unconditioned.

There is nothing in our mortal realm of flux, uncertainty and unhappiness that corresponds, even remotely, to these attributes. They are quite deliberately depicted as having metaphysical qualities to suggest the strongest possible contrast to our situation in this life. However, this same reality is closer to us than we can possibly imagine because, from its side, there is no separation whatsoever.

A conclusion we can reach is that this world is, in some respects, a distorted image of a more wondrous reality that cannot be fully realised in this life and of which the ubiquity of suffering is a continual reminder.

Its unsatisfactory nature reflects an estrangement from our origin while the joys we do find in it reveal Nirvana's luminous presence at the core of everyday life, inciting us to pursue a higher awakening. Evil is a consequence of living in a flawed reality that is evidently not the realm of bliss; having said that, this world is not entirely bereft of its light either.

The fact that suffering is so universal is no reason to doubt the reality of Nirvana—our very capacity to recognise suffering as such, and to want to free ourselves from it, is proof enough of its opposite.

Those occasions in life when we are confronted with an experience of overwhelming love or beauty are, in truth, the irresistible traces of Nirvana's unspeakable bliss in our mundane world. A renowned Buddhist master once declared that "What is beautiful partakes of the Buddha" and we can surely see why this must be so.

Such encounters serve as a reminder of the incomparable splendour of true reality that lies beyond our brittle natures; yet they can also present a painful contrast to the destitution we feel when cut off from Amida.

Many people today feel lonely and isolated. Like frightened motherless children, we desperately need to be loved and want to be appreciated by others but there is much self-dissatisfaction in this quest.

We mistake our blind reactions of attraction and repulsion for real life when, in fact, we have fallen into a benighted condition, being led merely by our emotions and sense experience. There is no illumined awareness here and, because we are drowning in burdensome subjectivity, there can be no freedom in this either.

Being exclusively engrossed with ourselves coarsens us and magnifies our imagined self-importance, leaving us in a state of perpetual combat with the world as we continue to reinforce a separate existence from others. This serves to make us feel 'special' which, in turn, rapidly fuels an attitude of unhealthy self-love.

The problem is that we are imprisoned by our restricted personalities. Spiritual ignorance is not just being uninformed of facts but rather being lost in ourselves, which signals an absence of light. Now, you might think that this is the last place you would expect to find Amida but it is precisely at such a low ebb in our lives that the 'true and real' is most within reach.

As the reality of Amida's life is never away from us, a transition takes place as we learn to rest in the cradle of Other-Power, regardless of the emotional upheavals that bedevil us. In allowing ourselves to be willingly filled and governed by this reality, our thoughtless responses to life start to decrease and we cease our senseless strife with others.

The transforming presence of shinjin graciously intrudes into and stabilises our anxious hearts. In this way, Amida becomes the true parent to all beings.

When the hard shell of our suffocating self-enclosure is cracked open by Amida, we undergo a change without actually doing anything other being attentive and fully receptive—through deep hearing—to this awareness that is freely given to us. Our cold hearts start to melt as we lose ourselves in this all-encompassing embrace that urges us to surrender to it.

As a result, we come to see ourselves in a more objective light that has nothing to do with our self-regard and which gives us the strength to face the vexations of life with greater confidence. Furthermore, we naturally acquire the virtues of humility, self-control, contentment and simplicity as we come to see the extent of our spiritual powerlessness. This is the basis for a truly contemplative life.

We are no longer shaken by hurt, guilt or a sense of inferiority and we neither dramatise nor suppress our feelings. Thanks to the working of Other-Power, we are able to remain spiritually firm in the face of our trials without self-condemnation.

The Primal Vow seeks to make us 'soft and gentle in body and mind' and this can have a salutary effect on relations with our fellows. In the light of its wisdom, we come to realise that we can never truly love selflessly and yet we see, at the same time, that Amida's love and concern for all sentient beings (in contrast to our own) is completely unconditional.

In fact, the love and care we wish—in our nobler moments—to bestow on others cannot actually have its foundation in the ego but only in the presence of Amida's light working in our hearts.

When this powerful insight is given to us, what do you suppose that does to our corrosive hatred of others? It must surely incline us towards a tender goodwill directed at everyone.

One is often asked whether prayer has any role to play in Shin Buddhism. It is certainly true that petitionary prayer is not practised in the sense of requesting favours or special treatment, especially in securing worldly goods. These things are subject to both the operation of karma as well as our own skill and initiative—though they can easily be taken by fortune—and should not be seen as divine gifts.

But may we request *spiritual* benefits? This would imply that these can only be received if asked for but the fact is that they are always being offered without the necessity for supplication. Amida's sole desire is to shower all beings, unreservedly, with every spiritual blessing if we could only but appreciate our need for them. And yet, in this sense, the natural human impulse to ask for help can already be seen as evidence of our willingness to receive such gifts, which are ever available to us.

The classical Indian texts (or sutras), on which this tradition is founded, aim to present the spiritual realities discussed in this work in the form of an accessible parable. They tell us that Amida was originally a king who gave up his throne to become a monk, called Dharmakara, in order to save all beings.

He vowed to do this by undertaking aeons of practice that would give him the unsurpassable merit to create a blissful realm—the Pure Land—to which we could go, after death, to continue our practice towards Nirvana without any suffering and under much more favourable conditions. In doing so, he vowed that he would not attain Buddhahood unless his desire to liberate suffering humanity came to fruition in this way.

The story goes on to say that, as a result of the enormous merit accumulated, he fulfilled his vows and became an enlightened Buddha called Amida, which is the Japanese contraction of the Sanskrit names *Amitabha* ('Light without end') and *Amitayus* ('Life without measure').

But instead of living in the world like the historical Buddha, Shakyamuni, he now presides over the Pure Land that was created for the sake of ordinary beings who could enter there by confidently invoking Amida's Name with faith and an aspiration for Nirvana.

Many, these days, cannot accept this story as true and see it only as a metaphorical window through which we can contemplate the light of eternal reality and its workings. On the other hand, there are those who can only bring themselves to believe in it if it did take place in some sense. This is the confrontation that many religions face today between a traditional and a modern interpretation of ancient scriptures.

The traditional view, having held sway for many centuries, has nurtured millions of faithful souls who clearly had no difficulty in believing its claims. This majestic story has immense power and is a very moving account of what compassion, on a cosmic scale, really means in tangible terms. Therefore, it should never be looked down on or belittled as a concession to inferior minds, for the spiritual certitudes it contains are very real and of the utmost importance, even if they are not considered historically factual.

Given that many who find themselves attracted to Shin Buddhism see Amida as being unbounded, it is difficult for them to conceive of this reality as having an origin in time, whether in our world or any other. This is quite understandable as it would impose a limit on what the tradition considers to be 'immeasurable'.

One way to view the story, that may assist in better understanding its objectives, is to see it as an unveiling of otherwise hidden truths. What the sutra does is tell us something about the attributes of Amida which would not be obvious if we had, say, just a simple experience of this measureless Light and Life in our lives (as wonderful as that would be).

In other words, knowing that Amida is what sustains all genuine practice (Other-Power), actively pursues all beings to bring them home (the Primal Vow) and accepts us all without judgement or condemnation (unconditional compassion) are insights that can only be *revealed* to us by that reality itself.

A very effective and approachable way to do this is through a sacred story which then becomes an instrument by which to convey the deep-seated significance disclosed by these 'events'. As such, it ought not to be regarded as a comprehensive or accurate description of ultimate reality, for which we should refer to other more philosophical Buddhist texts dedicated to that matter.

Of course, an immediate encounter with it can suggest something about this marvellous presence (for example, that it is a true refuge where we find spiritual repose in our lives) but it cannot impart *everything* we need to know about its intentions. Those unique aspects of the Shin teaching, regarding the essence of Amida's will, needed to be made more explicit. This required the tradition to adopt a vehicle whereby these eternal verities could be unmistakably divulged to us.

In its enlightened foresight, it settled on a particular narrative that would be easier for ordinary people to apprehend. This meant having to relate timeless truths in terms of 'cause-and-effect' and embodying numinous realities in the guise of a quasi-historical account. Therefore, the motivation behind this 'saving means' (*upaya*) is not, in any way, an arbitrary human contrivance but the expression of Amida's profoundly loving wisdom.

By such means, the story becomes an indispensable medium by which we come to know the true nature of Amida, something that cannot be discovered in any other way. Thus, we shouldn't casually dismiss this account as 'mere myth'. Myths should not be seen as untrue just because they lack a firm historical foundation. Rather, given their other-worldly origin, such allegories are a powerful means of laying bare deep mysteries that cannot be effectively conveyed through rational, empirical or other forms of ordinary knowledge. In the end, the highest truth will resort to any expedient necessary to declare itself.

Shinran speaks of the monk Dharmakara as having emerged from 'the ocean of Suchness' in order to make known its great compassionate vows to rescue all beings. This suggests that while ultimate reality (the Dharma-Body) is eternal, Amida as its manifestation is not necessarily so; which is not to suggest that the spiritual potency of Amida is, in any way, limited.

In other words, the need for this inconceivable reality to take form as a living Buddha with whom we can commune, was in response to the existence of sentient beings who are in need of it; otherwise, the 'true and real' could never be known to us.

If there were no people, there would be no need for Amida, who is actually an expression of the Dharma-Body adapted to the needs of humanity—yet ultimate reality, in itself, abides ceaselessly regardless of whatever else happens to exist in our world of relativity.

So, while the power of the Primal Vow to reach out to us and transform our lives is unhindered, it only remains so to the extent that there is a requirement for Nirvana to show a 'personal' face and until such time as samsara has been exhausted of all suffering sentient beings.

We can see then that this sacred story is revealing facts that are essentially spiritual. This makes them immune from any doubts that might be raised against any actual events, from the distant past, that were claimed as real but have subsequently been proven false—this would be a very insecure foundation for any kind of belief.

On the other hand, the veracity of spiritual truths can only be confirmed by direct insight (*shinjin*) as disclosed to us by Other-Power and not through mere historical research.

In this sense, Amida is a real transcendental Buddha whose existence is grounded on the highest reality itself. This ought to put paid to the utterly misconceived notion that Amida is just a symbol of our shared interpersonal solidarity or that Other-Power is only the help we receive from others in day-to-day life or that the Pure Land is merely our hankering for an ideal community brought about by social justice.

Shinran would have been appalled by such reductionism and seen it as spiritually destructive. The desire to seek greater harmony amongst ourselves can, of course, arise from an awakening to shinjin but diminishing the reality of who Amida is to just a set of worldly objectives would be a complete travesty. The lesson in all this is that we need to take the tradition's own view of itself seriously or not engage with it at all.

In the traditional sutras, the Pure Land is described as a realm of marvellous sights and sounds that embody the teaching of Amida. In many ways, it resembles a kind of paradise but its purpose is not merely to please the senses.

The splendid delights that are depicted in these descriptions are framed in such a way as to attract and inspire suffering beings who seek release from the wretched conditions of our world. They are highly effective in this way because the Pure Land is spoken of as possessing the utmost felicity, while employing the imagery of the transient things we love in this world to heighten our aspiration for it.

While Shinran's predecessors considered the Pure Land as an undefiled realm from which one cannot fall back into this world and to which we go in order to perfect our practice towards Nirvana, his view went one step further. While he did not deny that there were superior dimensions to existence where we could flourish and advance in our awareness, he did not consider them our ultimate destination.

The *true* Pure Land, according to Shinran, was none other than Nirvana itself which cannot be described in any sensuous or conceptual manner. It is therefore not somewhere we go to consummate our spiritual disciplines because all true practice has already been fulfilled by Amida on our behalf.

According to this understanding, what the tradition calls 'birth in the Pure Land' doesn't just take place when we pass away. Of course, Nirvana as a permanent state is only possible after death when we are no longer impeded by the disturbances of our human condition.

But seeing as Shinran equated Nirvana with Buddha-nature, he discovered that this realm is present to us—right here where we find ourselves—when there is true entrusting, regardless of how confused or troubled we may be. Because this unending Light shines without impediment, it can overcome whatever personal obstacles seem insurmountable from our side. All it asks is that we offer up, without any hesitation, our overwhelming karmic hindrances to its transformational working.

In the attempt to find a single English term that captures the meaning of shinjin, *faith* has often been proposed. This has been vigorously disputed seeing as that word, for many, suggests holding to a set of beliefs based on mere hope rather than on reason or factual evidence.

Yet this is a limited understanding of faith which, in its original connotation, allows for a richer meaning that comes closer to the sense of having complete confidence in something and seeing it as dependable. A more complex appreciation of faith also reveals that—far from being something irrational based on wishful thinking—it is a form of perception that sees spiritual realities clearly such that we are possessed by a certainty that does not originate in anything to do with mere 'belief' devoid of knowledge or experience.

During the course of this study, we have seen that shinjin is a no mere human accomplishment related to intelligence, skill, virtue or cleverness on our part. As already stated, it's an awareness that we cannot create as it is the arising of Buddha-nature which we experience as Amida's mind illuminating our otherwise turbid personality.

It also has the power to completely renew us through the truth it reveals by means of a spiritual knowledge that is vivid and unmediated. This awareness, having taken root in our hearts, will then blossom into the final emancipation in the Land of Bliss that is promised to us without first having to quell our binding desires, which make us so dependent on the world for our happiness. Even so, the gradual exposure of such desires to the wisdom of this immeasurable light will make us see what they've always really been aiming for, thus revealing to us the spiritual basis of all desire.

In Shin Buddhism, faith is understood as a loving union of hearts and not a baseless hope, for it is Other-Power alone that dispels doubt. This is a deep trust that can only flourish on the back of a visceral acquaintance with this reality.

Naturally, we cannot summon the strength that is required to sustain such trust if we are relying on our own resources. The great peace that comes with this faith (which belongs to Amida, not us) can only be taken as a gift that we accept with a heart of gladness.

The Primal Vow (*hongan*) is the fundamental desire behind the activity of Other-Power in our lives. It is a conscious will that ardently seeks to pursue and seize us without ever letting go. This empowering and insistent force thirsts for our freedom from samsara—it is ever at hand and tirelessly works to have us entrust ourselves to it. In this way, Amida is never distant from us. No greater compassion can be conceived than this unreserved longing to make us whole and set us free.

Earlier in this work, mention was made of the nembutsu as the encounter between Amida and ourselves in whatever condition we happen to be in. Some further remarks might be useful in gaining a clearer picture of this very important notion.

"Hearing the name of Amida and conceiving joyous faith" is a theme that runs right through the scriptures of this tradition. While it may sound odd at first, this expression describes the pivotal moment in which the 'deep mind' of shinjin is given to us.

Nembutsu is a Japanese word that means to keep the Buddha in one's thoughts. Indeed, a long-established and venerable practice has been to simply concentrate on a transcendental Buddha. This could include visualising, say, Amida's 'physical' form as metaphorically described in the sutras or—as became very popular over time—simply saying "I take refuge in the Buddha of immeasurable Light and Life" (*Namo Amida Butsu*).

This invocation eventually came to be almost synonymous with the nembutsu, although its purely mental form was never neglected. Indeed, one can hardly give verbal embodiment to one's devotion without also thinking on the Buddha (or, in a deeper sense, without the Buddha thinking of us).

So while the true Buddha in this tradition is known as Amida, the formal Name comprises the words in the invocation mentioned above. This is because it was felt important to capture the dynamic relationship between ourselves, in the act of taking refuge (which is the meaning of *Namo*), and Amida as the catalyst behind this awakening.

Therefore, to 'hear the Name' is to understand the meaning that is conveyed by *Namo Amida Butsu*. According to Shinran, the reason why we 'conceive joyous faith' in hearing it is because we are shown that all beings are enfolded in a tremendous light that radiates its wisdom and compassion inexhaustibly. We come to see that we are the object of its concern and that it wishes to deliver us from our spiritual desolation and estrangement.

When brought to this realisation, we naturally feel the need to express it and thus respond to the call of Amida by saying the Name with gratitude.

In other words, the nembutsu becomes the vocalisation of a momentous existential transformation that takes over our lives. This, in turn, informs our acts of service in the world which we undertake, instinctively, without pride and in a spirit of sharing the Dharma with others. As an old Japanese saying observes: "Where there is a flame of faith within, it will show itself in the smoke of conduct without".

When understood in this way, saying the nembutsu is clearly not something we do in order to achieve a particular spiritual goal. What is significant is that Shinran called it 'great practice', precisely because it is the work of Amida and not that of 'foolish beings' as the sutras describes us. This means that our saying of the Name emerges as the vehicle through which Other-Power grace becomes alive in us. To this end, remembrance of Amida may facilitate deep hearing if approached with an open heart and without expectations of any result or reward.

What, then, can we possibly contribute to the virtue of Other-Power? When it dawns on us that our own merits count for little and that we cannot solve our own spiritual problems without the aid of an all-pervading universal wisdom, we naturally come to abandon all self-working and petty calculation.

By way of conclusion and summary, let us now bring together the major features of Shinran's vision.

There is an ultimate reality that is the underlying essence of mind and matter—the self-sufficient source of all existence. This is known as the Dharma-Body which, in the final analysis, is all there is. While inconceivable in itself, it confers the light by which all things are known and perceived.

The intelligence inherent in the Dharma-Body is necessarily reflected in the complexity, order, intelligibility and beauty in the world (despite its many flaws which are inevitable) as well as in the aston-ishing intellectual and spiritual faculties of human beings who are uniquely placed to intimately share in the divine life of this reality.

Nirvana can be considered the Dharma-Body as experienced. It is a state of indescribable joy and imperishable peace that spells the end of all affliction, craving, rebirth and, of course, karma, which can no longer be accumulated. It is also the final fulfillment of all the long-ing we feel in this life (even unconsciously) for that reality, which is the only good that is absolute and permanent. In Nirvana, sickness, old age and death can no longer touch us as we will have forever relinquished the debilitating burdens of human life.

This ultimate reality also dwells in us as our deepest ground beyond anything that we think of as our everyday self and its egocentric com-pulsions. This is the Buddha-nature that is present in every sentient being as a trans-individual reality, although not disclosed in each of them equally. But inasmuch as it is also found deep within all things, it has assumed form as the external world which it wears and sheds like an outer garment.

So despite the varied forms of our distinctive personalities, we are united by virtue of our shared Buddha-nature. To use a traditional analogy, a body of water and the waves it generates are not separate even though the waves emerge in many different forms; yet, in the absence of any water, waves could not exist.

Amida has emerged from formless reality to assume an unambigu-ous form for our sake so that we can recognise and accept the spiri-tual gifts that are never withheld from us. While the Dharma-Body is not a mere 'person'—seeing as it exceeds every limitation suggested by that word—neither is it impersonal like some inanimate force or object; otherwise, it could never give rise to supreme compassion in the form of Amida as perfected personality. The phenomenon of per-sonhood is, arguably, one of the most remarkable realities in our existence and demands an explanation that does justice to its far-reaching metaphysical significance.

It is important to be aware that 'immortality' is not something attained by an individual like ourselves who happens to live forever.

Rather, it is an all-embracing life in which every hindrance that separates us from each other falls away in a dimension that is deathless.

When our karma has sufficiently matured, we hear the Name of Amida and understand that it is calling us, as Shinran urged, to 'abandon this old dwelling-place of pain' where there is just a futile repetition of birth and death without end. This realisation brings about a natural detachment which, in turn, delivers us from the slavery of being bound by desire, ignorance, anger and dread. In doing so, we stop clashing with life and come to settle, with unresisting ease, in the warm lap of Other-Power.

When shinjin—incorruptible like a white lotus flower—arises in us we are emancipated, even in this life, from the despotic oppression of our ego and its endless provocations. Amida, as the channel of spiritual power inherent in the Dharma-Body, is able to confer this enduring spiritual freedom to all who seek it.

As already mentioned, Shinran acknowledged that we do not always feel the joy or gratitude that ought to accompany such liberation. This he attributed to the powerful hold that our disordered impulses have over us. These never abate as long as we live but, because we see them for what they are through the eyes of Amida, we do not allow ourselves to stray for long before returning to the secure fortress of the Primal Vow.

We end our reflections by leaving the final word with Shinran who has been our trusted guide and friend throughout this journey. May his uplifting vision of what it means to be truly alive inspire us all to seek refuge in the ever-beckoning light of Amida and return home.

"Those who attain true and real shinjin ... necessarily attain Nirvana. ... To attain Nirvana is to attain eternal bliss. Eternal bliss is ultimate tranquility."

The author is a Shin Buddhist priest from Australia. His previous works include *Call of the Infinite*, *The Fragrance of Light* and *The Unhindered Path*.

Made in the USA
Monee, IL
31 December 2020